Kid's Box

Kid's Box reports

Activity Book 6

Caroline Nixon & Michael Tomlinson

High technology

1 Choose words from the box to complete the text.

excited	going	~~started~~	thirtieth	Maths
won	laughed	horrible	year	something

The kids (1) _started_ back at school last week and they're ready for another (2) _____ of study. They're really (3) _____ about working on *Kid's Box* again, their ezine for young people. Last year they (4) _____ the school prize for the best project and this year they want to win an international ezine competition if they can. They're (5) _____ to visit lots of places and write about some very interesting things. Last Wednesday they met to talk about their new project and they also looked at some funny photos from last year. They (6) _____ a lot when they remembered some of the things that happened.

2 Correct the sentences.

1 The kids started their holidays last week. _The kids started back at school last week._
2 They're ready for another month of study. _____
3 They won the school prize for Art. _____
4 They met last Friday. _____
5 They watched some funny DVDs. _____
6 They cried a lot when they remembered. _____

3 Write sentences.

1 **2** **3** **4** **5** **6**

1 _We use a toothbrush to clean our teeth._   4 _____
2 _____   5 _____
3 _____   6 _____

4 Answer the questions.

1 What did you do during the holidays? _____
2 Where did you go? _____
3 Who did you see? _____
4 What did you eat? _____
5 What did you do? _____
6 Who were you with? _____

5 Put the words in groups.

| ~~Maths~~ ~~friendly~~ ~~pizza~~ Geography excited afraid salt English |
| bored salad surprised sandwich History pepper Science |

How we feel

friendly _____

_____

_____

_____

_____

What we eat

pizza _____

_____

_____

_____

_____

Things we study

MON	Maths _____
TUES	_____
WEDS	_____
THURS	_____
FRI	_____

6 Find the letters on the clock. Make words.

1 It's twenty-five to twelve. wing _____
2 It's twenty-five past six. _____
3 It's twenty to eleven. _____
4 It's ten past one. _____
5 It's ten to nine. _____

7 Write times to make four more words.
You can use the same letters again.

1 It's ten to eleven. (doll) _____
2 _____
3 _____
4 _____

8 Find and write the adjectives.

iped

ired

ot

errible

mous

orrible

ong

~~fraid~~

a**fraid** _____
a_____
fa_____
fa_____
da_____
da_____
s_____
s_____

h_____
h_____
lo_____
lo_____
str_____
str_____
t_____
t_____

ngerous

rk

t

vely

oft

wake

quare

ud

9 Sort and write the words. Label the pictures.

~~bakydroc~~   nep irved   cawmeb   corphimneo   adephoshen   toppla

1 _____ **2** _____ **3** _____ **4** _____ **5** _____ **6** __keyboard__ ____

10 Correct the sentences.

1 A laptop is a big, heavy computer which we can't carry in a special bag.
__A laptop is a small.__ _____

2 Speakers are like microphones. We use both of them to see our friends when we chat with them.
_____

3 The whiteboard is the part of the computer which has the letters and numbers. We use it to draw.
_____

4 We use a microphone to carry information from one computer to another.
_____

11 Which computer should Peter buy? Tick (✓) the correct box.

Peter needs a new computer because the one he has got is very old. The CD player doesn't work so he can't listen to music. It hasn't got a DVD player but he isn't unhappy because he doesn't like films. He has a lot of problems with his old computer when he tries to use the Internet because it is too slow. The Internet is important for him because he uses it to get information for his school projects. He also uses his computer a lot to write and chat with his friends, but he never uses it to play games. He doesn't need to carry his computer when he travels so he doesn't want a laptop. He thinks it's a good idea to change his pen drive too because he uses that to take his projects and songs round to his friend's house.

The KB4
Speakers
DVD player
Big screen - great for playing games
Special keyboard
£425

The KB5
Laptop computer
DVD player
Speakers
Better memory
Good for the Internet   **£350**

The KB6
FREE!
CD player
CD player
Webcam
Microphone
Speakers
Good for the Internet
Free pen drive
£395

12 Write three reasons why you chose that computer in your notebook.

13 Join two words to make one. Write the new word.

1 home   ball   _____
2 head   board   _____
3 key   room   _____
4 class   work   **homework**
5 basket   phones   _____

14 Write another word at the end to make new words.

1 bath**room**_____   3 fire_____   5 arm_____   7 foot_____
2 book_____   4 hand_____   6 tooth_____   8 snow_____

15 Find eight differences.

In Picture A, the boy's chatting online. In Picture B, he's watching a film. _____

_____

_____

_____

_____

_____

_____

_____

16 Answer the questions.

1 Can you use a computer? _____
2 Do you write emails? _____
3 Do you chat with your friends on the Internet? _____
4 Have you or your parents got a computer? _____
5 Do you use pen drives? _____
6 Do you write text messages to your friends? _____
7 Where do you listen to music? _____
8 Do you prefer headphones or speakers? _____

17 Say the chant and <u>underline</u> the stressed words.

<u>boys</u>	˙eat	sweets
the boys	eat	sweets
the boys	eat my	sweets
the boys will	eat my	sweets

18 Now complete the table with words from the chant.

Content words (nouns, main verbs)	Function words (articles, auxiliary verbs, adjectives)
<u>boys</u> _____	_____
_____	_____
_____	_____

Which words are stressed: content words or function words? _____

Lst wknd ptr wnt 2 hs uncls hs in the cntry. Hs uncl lvs on a frm. Hs a frmr. Ptr hlpd hm wth the anmls. He gt up erly and gt the mlk frm the cws, n the egs frm the chckns. Thrs a smll drty lak on the frm n ptr fll in2 it. lol.

◄ **Write it right**

When we use text language:
- We take out the vowels:
  clssrm – classroom
- We use words or letters that sound the same, but are shorter:
  hw r u (= How are you?)
- Some people don't use punctuation or capital letters in a short message.

19 Write the text above correctly.

Last weekend
_____
_____
_____
_____
_____
_____
_____
_____
_____

20 Write a text message for your friend to read.

----

21 Read and answer.

1 What time's Diggory giving his talk?
At half past two.

2 What kind of computer has Diggory got?

3 What can he use to explain ancient Maths and technology?

4 Who's Sir Doug Bones?

5 Why does he want to look under the cloth?

6 Who's got the calendar at the end?

22 Look at the code. Write the secret message.

A	B	C	D	E	F	G	H	I	J	K	L	M

N	O	P	Q	R	S	T	U	V	W	X	Y	Z

The _____ _____ _____

_____ _____ _____ _____

_____ _____ _____ .

Do you remember?

1   10.55 is five **to** _____ eleven.

2   _____ don't we buy a new computer?

3   I bought a _____ , so now I can see my friends when we talk on the computer.

4   A small computer which we can carry easily is a _____ .

5   When we say 'fish and chips', we don't stress the word _____ .

6   In text language 'U' means _____ .

Can do   I can name the parts of a computer.

I can talk about technology.

I can write text messages in English.

Going to

We use *going to* to talk about plans.

Affirmative	Negative (n't = not)	Question
I'm (am) going to read.	You **aren't going to** listen to music.	**Is** he **going to** play tennis?
She**'s (is) going to** read.	We **aren't going to** listen to music.	**Are** they **going to** play tennis?
We**'re (are) going to** read.	He **isn't going to** listen to music.	**Am** I **going to** play tennis?

1 Correct the sentences.

1 I're going to be in the play. I'm going to be in the play.
2 She's going be the lion. _____
3 Do you are going to watch *The Lion King*? _____
4 They isn't going to go to the theatre tomorrow. _____
5 What has he going to do at the weekend? _____
6 She hasn't going to wash her hair today. _____

2 Complete the questions. Match them with the answers.

Who	~~Which~~	Where	When	Why	What

1 **Which** _____ bus are you going to catch?
2 _____ are we going to play football?
3 _____ is he going to call?
4 _____ is she going to wash the car?
5 _____ is he going to read?
6 _____ are they going to do the exam?

a He's going to call his mum. ☐
b They're going to do it tomorrow. ☐
c He's going to read his comic. ☐
d I'm going to catch the number 27. ☐ 1
e In the park. ☐
f Because it's dirty. ☐

3 Look at the code. Write the secret message.

H	I	J	K	L	M	N	O	P	Q	R	S	T	U	V	W	X	Y	Z	A	B	C	D	E	F	G
A	B	C	D	E	F	G	H	I	J	K	L	M	N	O	P	Q	R	S	T	U	V	W	X	Y	Z

AOL AOLHAYL JSBI PZ NVPUN AV ZOVD AOL WSHF

The _____ ____ __ _____ __ _____ ___ ____

VU AOL SHZA AOBYZKHF HUK MYPKHF VM QBUL.

__ ___ ____ _____ ___ _____ __ ____.

4 Find six sentences and write them in your notebook.

He isn't	tickets	to rain	animals.
How many	to get	eat	tomorrow.
Are they going	going	do you	monkey.
They didn't	isn't going	for the	an actor.
Lions	choose him	to be	the play?
It	catch and	parts in	want?

5 What are they going to do?

1 Robert's switching on the TV.
   <u>He's going to watch TV.</u> _____

2 Sue's standing outside the castle and she's holding her camera.
   _____

3 The car's very dirty. Mr White is walking towards it with some water.
   _____

4 Some people are standing at the bus stop.
   _____

5 The boys are walking to the park. They're carrying a football.
   _____

6 There's some paper in front of Emma and she's picking up a pen.
   _____

6 Think about January next year. Answer the questions.

1 How old are you going to be? _____
2 What class are you going to be in at school? _____
3 Which subjects are you going to study? _____
4 Which clubs are you going to join? _____
5 What are you going to do after school and on which days? _____
6 Which books are you going to read? _____
7 Which films are you going to see? _____
8 What else are you going to do? _____

7 Use your answers to write about what you're going to do next year.

> <u>In January next year, I'm going to be</u> _____
> _____
> _____
> _____
> _____

8 Find the words. Label the picture.

f	a	i	r	i	e	n
n	e	s	t	o	s	h
a	a	a	u	e	c	o
o	g	g	t	e	a	r
e	l	a	o	h	l	n
f	e	e	o	u	e	f
c	l	a	w	u	s	r

1 _____

2 _____

3 *eagle* _____

4 _____ **5** _____ **6** _____

9 Look at the other letters in the wordsearch in Activity 8. Cross out all the vowels which aren't 'i'. Write the other letters. _____

Which beast is it? _____

10 Correct the sentences.

1 The dragon's got fur on its body. <u>The dragon's got scales on its body.</u> _____

2 The dragon wants to get the parrot's eggs. _____

3 The dragon and the eagle have got dangerous hands. _____

4 The dragon's got feathers on its wings, but the eagle hasn't. _____

5 The dragon's got two ears on its head. _____

6 The eagle's eggs are in a cave. _____

11 Look at these beasts. Invent names and describe them.

1 <u>This is a 'Dinolion'.</u>
<u>It's got a dinosaur's</u> _____
_____
_____
_____

2 _____
_____
_____
_____

3 _____
_____
_____
_____

12 Read and answer 'yes' or 'no'.

The Sphinx existed in Ancient Egyptian and Ancient Greek mythology. In Greek mythology the Sphinx had a lion's body, legs and claws, a snake's tail, eagle's wings and a woman's head. The story says that she sat at the door of the ancient city of Thebes to guard it. To go into the city people had to answer the Sphinx's question. If they got it right, they could go into the city. If they got it wrong, she ate them. The Ancient Greek writer, Sophocles, wrote the question in his work. It was 'Which creature goes on four feet in the morning, two feet in the afternoon and three feet in the evening?' Do you know the answer?

1 The Sphinx was a real animal. **no** _____
2 She had a bird's wings. _____
3 She had a mammal's tail. _____

4 She stood at the door of Thebes. _____
5 She asked people a question. _____
6 People who didn't know went home. _____

13 Write the words.

1 an ancient story about heroes = **myth** _____
2 snakes have got these on their bodies = _____
3 birds have these on their wings = _____
4 a word for animal or creature = _____
5 a very expensive yellow metal = _____
6 some birds make these in trees = _____
7 the home of a king or queen = _____
8 half woman, half fish = _____

14 Now cross out the first letter of each answer in Activity 13. Read the other letters to answer the Sphinx's question.

n	g	a	~~m~~	f	m
c	m	s	b	a	n

— — — —

15 What's going to happen?

The boat is going to break on the rocks. _____ _____ _____

_____ _____
_____ _____

11

16 Say the sentences quickly. <u>Underline</u> the sounds that are missing or different when we speak quickly.

1   She put it o<u>n m</u>y leg.
2   Can I try that cake, please?
3   She's a good girl.

4   I love sand castles.
5   Those are nice shoes.
6   Let's go in that dress shop.

17 Complete the story with 'who', 'where' or 'which'.

This is the myth of Icarus, the boy
(1) who___ flew too near to the Sun
and fell out of the sky. Daedalus,
(2) _____ was Icarus' father, was
a clever artist. Minos, (3) _____
was the King of Crete, asked him to make
a labyrinth (4) _____ was very
difficult to get out of. The labyrinth was
the place (5) _____ a terrible
beast called the Minotaur lived.

Write it right

Writing longer sentences

Join sentences with **who**, **where** and **which**.

Sophocles was a writer. He wrote the Sphinx's question in his work.
→ Sophocles, **who** was a writer, wrote the Sphinx's question in his work.

The nests are made of gold. Griffins live in them.
→ The nests **where** griffins live are made of gold.

A dragon is a beast. It has scales and big claws.
→ A dragon is a beast **which** has scales and big claws.

18 Now write the rest of the story correctly. Use 'who', 'where' or 'which'.

Theseus, who _____
_____
_____
_____
_____
_____
_____
_____
_____
_____
_____
_____
_____
_____

Theseus, / was the son of the King of Athens, decided to save the children from the beast.

Ariadne, / was King Minos' daughter, gave Theseus some string / he used when he went into the labyrinth.

Theseus went into the place / the beast lived and killed it. The string / Ariadne gave him helped him to find the way out.

King Minos was very angry with Daedalus because he was the man / gave Ariadne the string.

He sent Daedalus to Crete, a small island / he had to stay with his son, Icarus.

Daedalus made some wings / he used to escape from Crete with his son. Icarus felt very happy and flew too near the Sun, / burnt his wings and feathers.

Today the place / Icarus fell into the sea is an island / is called Icaria.

19 Read and answer.

1 Where's the Aztec calendar from? A museum in Mexico City.

2 Who's Iyam Greedy? _____

3 How do you write 6 in the Mayan Maths system? _____

4 Who was Quetzalcoatl? _____

5 What's in the email? _____

6 Where are Diggory and Emily going to go? _____

20 Complete and match.

1 How am I going to tell the museum in Mexico City? [d]

2 A spot means one and a _____ means five. □

3 It _____ like a phone number to me. □

4 I'm a snake and I've got _____ . □

5 He was part _____ and part snake. □

Do you remember?

1 They aren't going _____ to choose Dan for the part of the monkey.

2 They are going _____ write about exciting beasts.

3 Dragons have got _____ on their bodies.

4 Eagles live in _____ in high places.

5 Griffins had an eagle ____ head and the body and back legs _____ a lion.

6 The place _____ Icarus fell into the sea is now an island called Icaria.

Can do   I can talk about what is going to happen.

I can talk about beasts from myths and legends.

I can write a myth.

1 Read and order the text.

books and stories about the legend of a		2
he can't because he's very old.		
beautiful, strong woman called Hua Mu Lan.		
There's a film about		
Hua Mu Lan's adventures, but in the		
Do you know this film? Do you like it?		
In this story Hua Mu Lan's		
to help China in her father's place.		
of men to save China, but		
film she's called Fa Mulan.		
In China there are a lot of		1
puts on her brother's clothes.		
She takes her father's horse and goes		
father has to go with a group		
To help her father, Hua Mu Lan cuts her hair and		

2 Write the story in your notebook.

3 Read and choose the right words.

Another legend which is in a lot of films is about King Arthur. **(1)** (He) / **Him** was an English king hundreds of years ago. Arthur became the King when he pulled a sword out of a stone. **(2) It / He** was very difficult and nobody else could do it. Arthur was King of England for a long time with his wife Guinevere. Arthur loved **(3) she / her** a lot. **(4) He / His** good friend, the magician Merlin, helped Arthur. He had a big, round table **(5) where / who** his 12 knights sat. They helped Arthur look **(6) at / after** England.

4 Write about a legend from your country.

1 Think about the name of the hero. _____

2 What did he/she do? _____

3 Who did he/she do it with? _____

4 Why is he/she famous? _____

----

5 Choose words from the box to complete the text.

lot	~~were~~	There	which	whose	was	so	who	many

Greek myths (1) _were__ full of gods and beasts. The 12 most important gods lived on the Mountain of Olympus. Each god was important for a different area of life. Zeus was very important because he was the King of the gods and was also the father of (2) _____ other gods and heroes. Other important gods were Aphrodite (the god of Love), Hades (the god of the Underworld), Athena (the god of the Arts), Apollo (the god of Music) and Poseidon (the Sea god). There were also a (3) _____ of different beasts in Greek myths. Some of the famous beasts are Gorgon, a monster who had a snake's head; the Chimera, who had three heads; Hydra, (4) _____ head grew again if someone cut it off; Pegasus, a horse which had wings; and the Cerberus, a dog with three heads. There were also dragons and sea snakes (5) _____ Greek heroes had a lot of things to worry about!

6 Read again and answer.

1 Who was the most important Greek god? Zeus._____
2 Who was Aphrodite? _____
3 Who was the god of Music? _____
4 What was special about Gorgon? _____
5 Which beast could fly? _____
6 What's the name of the dog with three heads? _____

7 Look at Unit 1 in your Pupil's Book and Activity Book. Make a list of Greek gods, beasts and heroes.

Gods	
Beasts	
Heroes	Jason,

8 My project

I did my project   at school ☐   at home ☐.
I worked   alone ☐   with a friend ☐   in a group ☐.
I had   lots of ☐   some ☐   no ☐   problems.
The project was   interesting ☐   OK ☐   boring ☐.
I want to remember: _____
_____

2 Tomorrow's world

Will

We use *will* to talk about the future.

Affirmative	Negative (won't = will not)	Question
I'll go to the Moon.	You **won't** travel by car.	**Will** she fly in a rocket?
It'll go to the Moon.	We **won't** travel by car.	**Will** they fly in a rocket?

1 Read and match.

1 People will have   a   invent a carplane. ☐
2 She won't go   b   will go to the Moon on holiday. ☐
3 NASA will send a   c   computers on their bicycles. [1]
4 There won't be any   d   solar satellite next year. ☐
5 Someone will   e   to school by bus. ☐
6 Some people   f   cars in a hundred years. ☐

2 Complete the chart. Tick (✓) 'Yes' or 'No'.

Will you …	Yes	No
1 travel to the Moon?		
2 have the same job as your parents?		
3 have lots of children?		
4 live in the same town as you live in now?		
5 go to university when you're older?		

3 Now write sentences with 'will' or 'won't'.
I will / won't travel to the Moon.

1
2
3
4
5

4 Read the notes. Complete the sentences.

9.00 Arrive at school. Change clothes for sports lesson.
9.15 Play badminton.
10.00 Have a shower.
10.30 Go to Maths lesson.
11.15 Go out to play. Drink some orange juice.

1 When Peter arrives at school, **he'll change his clothes for sport.**
2 After he plays badminton,
3 After he has Maths,
4 When he goes out to play,

16

5 Will these things happen in 2050? Write sentences with 'will' or 'won't'.

1 Children / classes / home <u>Children won't have classes at home.</u>
2 People / go / Mars _____
3 People / fly / cars _____
4 People / use computers _____
5 Children / have electronic books _____
6 People / use more plastic _____

6 Read and complete.

quickly	~~shower~~	won't	arms	cup	will	clean

This is my new invention to help children in the future. It's a cross between a (1) shower and a car-wash. It'll have two funny metal (2) _____ with big gloves made of rubber. These (3) _____ move round and round very (4) _____ to wash us with soap and water. One of them will (5) _____ our teeth with a toothbrush, too. Outside the shower there'll be a machine to dry us. It'll look like a big (6) _____ which we'll stand under. We'll have a shower and we (7) _____ have a wet towel.

7 Design and draw an invention to help children in the future.

8 Write about your invention.

9 Label the photos.

| engineer | astronaut | ~~tourist~~ | businessman |

tourist _____ _____ _____ _____

10 Sort and write the words.

1 Earth _____
2 _____   4 _____
3 _____   5 _____

11 Complete the sentences.

1 Space ____ is the name we give to everything outside Earth's air.
2 An _____ is a person who designs or makes machines or electrical things.
3 We breathe _____ .
4 The planet _____ is where we live.
5 An _____ can travel in space.
6 The _____ goes round our planet. We can see it at night.
7 A _____ visits another town or country on holiday.
8 A man who works in business is called a _____ .
9 A _____ goes very quickly and can take people into space.

12 Read and answer 'yes' or 'no'.

The Space Race started in 1957 when the Soviet Union sent a satellite into space. It was called Sputnik 1. A satellite is something which goes round Earth. The Soviet Union then sent a dog called Laika into space in Sputnik 2. Next, the USA sent its own satellite, called Explorer 1, into space. In 1958 the USA started their space agency called NASA. Three years later in 1961 the Russian Yuri Gagarin became the first astronaut to orbit Earth in a spaceship. It wasn't until July 1969 that the first person, Neil Armstrong, walked on the Moon.

1 The Soviet Union sent the first satellite into space. yes__
2 The first animal in space was a monkey. _____
3 The USA started NASA in 1959. _____
4 Yuri Gagarin was an astronaut from the USA. _____
5 Gagarin flew round Earth. _____
6 Neil Armstrong was the first man to walk on the Moon. _____

13 Match the ideas about life on Zeron, the space city. Write sentences.

1 telescopes in the windows   a to build new houses
2 satellites   b to get energy
3 solar panels   c to travel into space
4 robots   d to look at the stars
5 rockets   e to receive signals from space

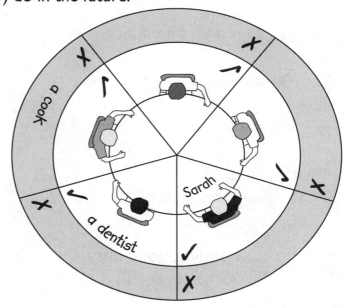

1

1 We'll have telescopes in the windows to look at the stars.
2 _____
3 _____
4 _____
5 _____

14 Read and answer the riddles.

1 The beginning of Earth, the end of space. The beginning of every end, the end of every place.
   What am I? 'e'. _____
2 What comes once in a minute, twice in a moment and never in a thousand years? _____
3 Which letter will come next in this sequence? M, A, M, J, J, A, S, O ... ? _____
4 How will you use the letters in NEW DOOR to make one word? _____
5 Harry was an engineer. His mother had four children. The first was April, the second was May
   and the third was June. What was the name of her fourth child? _____
6 A man's looking at a photo of a famous astronaut and he says, 'I have no brothers and sisters,
   but that man's father is my father's son.' Who's he looking at? _____

15 Read and complete the circle with names and jobs.

There are three girls and two boys. They're talking about
the jobs they think they will (✓) and won't (✗) do in the future.

1 Sarah's sitting between Dave and Mike.
   The person on Mike's left thinks she'll be
   an actress but she won't be a painter.
2 The boy who says he'll be a dentist won't
   be an actor.
3 The person on Mary's left won't be a
   photographer but she thinks she'll be
   a mechanic.
4 The girl next to Lucy loves cameras so she'll
   be a photographer, but she won't be a cook.
5 The boy next to Lucy loves rockets but he
   won't be an astronaut. He thinks he'll be a
   rocket engineer.

16 Read the Tourist Space Programme and answer.

Holidays in Space
Friday 17 July 2047

7:00	Meet at the Earth Space Station, Houston, Texas, USA.
8:00	Leave Earth in a spaceplane.
8.30	Stop at The Milky Way star café for breakfast (hot chocolate and cake pills).
9.30	Put on spacesuits. Get on the KB6 Adventurer space rocket.
12.00	Arrive on the Moon. Walk around and take photos.
12.30	Go to The Armstrong Moon restaurant for lunch (chicken salad in an envelope). Take off spacesuits to eat.
1.30	Catch a Moon bus to go to the space port.
2.00	Get on the KB6 Adventurer again. Fly to The Galactica Hotel.

1 How will they leave Earth?
   They'll leave Earth in a spaceplane.

2 Where will they stop for breakfast?
   ----

3 What will they have for breakfast?
   ----

4 What will they put on?
   ----

5 What will they do on the Moon before lunch?
   ----

6 Why will they take off their spacesuits?
   ----

17 Practise saying your answers with the "ll' form correctly.

Write it right ◄

Connectors
• Remember to use some of these words to join your sentences and sequence them: **When, Then, After that, because, before**

18 Use your answers to write the Space Programme in your notebook.

The tourists will meet at the Earth Space Station at seven o'clock. Then they'll leave Earth in a spaceplane at eight o'clock. Before they get on the KB6 Adventurer space rocket, they'll stop

19 Invent the rest of the Space Programme. How long will they stay? What will they do? How will they come home?

They'll --

----

20 Read and answer.

1 Why did Iyam Greedy send them tickets to Mexico City? <u>There are legends about Aztec gold.</u>
2 What did the Aztecs and the Mayas use to measure time? _____
3 When did the Aztec new year start? _____
4 What will be the longest day of the year? _____
5 What's the date now in the story? _____
6 Will they stay in Mexico City tonight? _____

21 Read and order the text. Write the story in your notebook.

technology and their ancient Maths system. Iyam Greedy, who's a pirate and ☐

notebook and talked about a group of stars. There was a man sitting next to them. He ☐

phone number for Diggory in a letter. When Diggory phoned the number, Iyam ☐

only wants to get the Aztec gold and be rich, stole the Sun Stone and left a ☐

Diggory Bones is an archaeologist who teaches at City University. He had the [1]

On the plane to Mexico City, Diggory and his daughter, Emily, looked at a ☐

man from the plane got into a car with Iyam Greedy and followed their bus. ☐

listened to them talking. When Diggory and Emily caught a bus to Teotihuacan, the ☐

talked about Aztec mythology. Then he sent him two plane tickets in an email. ☐

Sun Stone. This is the name for the Aztec calendar, which he had to talk about Mayan (and Aztec) ☐

Do you remember?

1 In the future there <u>will</u> _____ be spaceplanes.
2 That's not a very good paper plane. It _____ fly very far.
3 _____ are people who fly in space in their job.
4 Our planet is called _____ .
5 In the question 'When'll they arrive?', ''ll' is a contraction of _____ .
6 _____ they build a spaceplane for tourists, we'll fly round Earth on our holiday.

Can do I can talk about what will happen.
I can talk about travel in the future.
I can write about space travel.

21

1 Sort the words. Write the planets and dwarf planets.

①  u a r t S n

②  a M s r

③ N t n u e e P

④  c e M r r y u

⑤  r a t h E

⑥  r a U u s n

_Saturn_____   _____   _____   _____   _____   _____

⑦ V u e s n

⑧ p i u J r e t

⑨ u l P o t

⑩ e C r s e

⑪ s r E i

_____   _____   _____   _____   _____

2 Write the planets in order (1 = closest to the Sun).

1 _Mercury_____   2 _____   3 _____   4 _____

5 _____   6 _____   7 _____   8 _____

3 Complete the sentences.

1 Earth is the **third**_____ planet from the Sun.

2 _____ is the smallest planet.

3 _____ is the biggest planet.

4 The planets _____ the Sun. This means that they move around it.

5 Earth moves around the Sun once every _____ .

4 Read and answer 'yes' or 'no'.

Satellites

The Moon is a natural satellite of Earth. A satellite is something which orbits a planet. Today space agencies send many other satellites into orbit. They use them for a lot of different things. We all know that they use satellites for TV communications. Television channels send the pictures to the satellites so that people can see the programmes all over the world. Telephone companies also use satellites so we can talk to people in different countries. Weather satellites are important to us too. Scientists use them to tell us what tomorrow's weather will be like.

1 Earth is a satellite of the Moon. **no**___

2 A satellite goes round a planet. _____

3 There are a lot of satellites which orbit Earth. _____

4 TV channels use satellites to make programmes. _____

5 Telephone companies don't use satellites. _____

6 Scientists use satellite pictures to say what the weather will be like. _____

22

5 Read and complete the factfile.

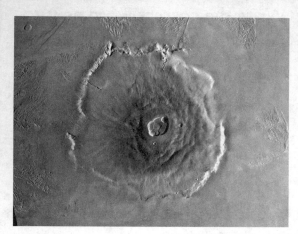

Mars is the fourth planet from the Sun and is often called the Red Planet. Mars takes 687 days to go round the Sun, so on Mars a year is 687 days long.

Mars has two moons. It also has the biggest volcanic mountain in the solar system. This is called Olympus Mons. It is 27 km high and it has a diameter of 600 km. There are no rivers or lakes on Mars so scientists think there is no life there, but they think it's possible that there's water under the ground. They want to send astronauts to Mars to look at the rocks and to look for water.

FACTFILE – PLANETS

Planet: Mars

Position from the Sun: _____

Other name: _____

Orbits the Sun every: _____

How many moons: _____

Interesting facts: _____

_____

_____

_____

_____

_____

_____

_____

6 Write about Neptune in your notebook.

FACTFILE – PLANETS

Planet: Neptune

Position from the Sun: eighth

Orbits the Sun every: 165 years

How many moons: eight

Interesting facts:
• strongest winds (2,000 km/h)
• has five rings
• coldest planet

7 Complete the sentences.

1 The Sun is 149.6_____ million km from Earth.

2 A day on Saturn is _____ hours.

3 _____ has the longest days.

4 _____ has the biggest volcano.

5 The Sun gives us _____ and heat.

8 My project

I did my project   at school ☐   at home ☐.

I worked   alone ☐   with a friend ☐   in a group ☐.

I had   lots of ☐   some ☐   no ☐   problems.

The project was   interesting ☐   OK ☐   boring ☐.

I want to remember: _____

_____

Review Units 1 and 2

1 Read the story. Choose a word from the box. Write the correct word next to numbers 1–5.

> tomorrow   engineer   food   will   future   museum   ~~favourite~~   drive
> rocket   picture

Friendly

Friendly is the kids' **favourite** TV programme. It's a comedy and it's very funny. It's about five friends who all live and study in the same school. Last week the friends had an interview with a special teacher to talk about their (1) _____ jobs. They had to think about which school subjects they were good at, and where they wanted to work.

Sue wants to study Art at university. Jim loves sport and keeping fit and wants to be a firefighter. Peter loves (2) _____ and he says he'll be a cook. Sally says she'll be a taxi driver. Jenny's good at English and drama and wants to be an actor. She says that when she's famous, Sally (3) _____ drive her to the film studio, Peter will cook her lovely meals and Sue will paint her (4) _____ and put it in a big, important (5) _____ . When Jim asks what he'll do for her, Jenny says her house will never catch fire so he'll have to change his job!

2 Now choose the best name for the story.

Tick one box.   Past and present ☐   After-school club ☐   Future plans ☐

3 Read and match the jokes.

1	What's green and smells like paint?	a	The outside.	☐
2	How does a monster count to 13?	b	All of them can. A house can't jump.	☐
3	Which side of an eagle has the most feathers?	c	A purple carrot!	☐
4	What do you get if you cross a blue cat with a red parrot?	d	I don't know, but when it talks you should listen carefully!	☐
5	How many seconds are there in a year?	e	Green paint.	1
6	Which animal can jump higher than a house?	f	On its fingers!	☐
7	Where can you find a sea without water?	g	A road.	☐
8	Why don't mother kangaroos like rainy days?	h	On a map!	☐
9	What goes through towns and up and over hills, but doesn't move?	i	Twelve: January the second, February the second ...	☐
10	What do you get if you cross a parrot with a tiger?	j	Because their children have to play inside!	☐

4 Complete the sentences. Count and write the letters.

1 <u>Space</u> ____ is the place outside Earth's air, where the Moon and planets are. `5`

2 A griffin's nest is made of _____ .

3 In text language, 'tchnlgy' means _____ .

4 We breathe _____ . It's called 'wind' when it moves over Earth.

5 Somebody who works in space is an _____ .

6 Eagles have got lots of _____ on their wings.

7 A small, light computer that we can carry easily is a _____ .

8 'What _____ you do?' 'I'll ask Michael to help me.'

9 The Sun is the only _____ in our solar system.

10 The _____ is the part of the computer which has the letters which we use to write.

11 A space station uses a _____ to send astronauts into space.

12 An _____ designs cars and motorbikes.

13 We use a _____ to see our friends when we're chatting on the Internet.

14 _____ are at the end of a dragon's leg.

5 Write the words in the crossword. Write the message.

1	2	3	4		5	6		7	8	9	10
											s	?

6 Quiz time!

1 What toy animal did Dan have in the audition? <u>He had</u> _____

2 What was the name of Jason's boat? _____

3 Who fought the Minotaur? _____

4 How will tourists fly into space in the future? _____

5 Which planet is 'the Red Planet'? _____

6 How many moons has Saturn got? _____

7 Write questions for your quiz in your notebook.

3 The great outdoors

LOOK again

Past continuous

We use the *past continuous* to describe what was happening in the past.

Affirmative	Negative	Question
I **was climbing** when I fell.	I **wasn't walking**.	**Was** I **playing**?
You **were climbing** when you fell.	He **wasn't walking**.	**Was** she **playing**?
He **was climbing** when he fell.	They **weren't walking**.	**Were** we **playing**?

1 Read and match.

1 She was skating
2 We were cooking sausages
3 You were flying your kite
4 He was skiing down the hill fast
5 I was sleeping
6 They were waiting at the station

when

a   he saw a tree in front of him. ☐
b   it flew into a tree. ☐
c   she fell down. [1]
d   the kitchen caught fire. ☐
e   their train arrived. ☐
f   you phoned me. ☐

2 Look at the pictures. Answer the questions.

1   Was Betty playing volleyball at quarter past eleven? <u>Yes, she was.</u>
2   Were Frank and Betty doing their homework at quarter past five? _____
3   Was Frank playing the guitar at ten past seven? _____
4   Were Frank and Betty having lunch at twenty-five past one? _____
5   Was Betty cleaning her teeth at half past eight? _____
6   Were Frank and Betty watching TV at ten to five? _____

3 Write four more questions about Frank and Betty in your notebook.

4 Correct two mistakes in each sentence.

1   Richard was ~~run~~ for the bus when he ~~dropping~~ his bag. <u>running, dropped</u>
2   Peter and Fred was playing baseball when it start to rain. _____
3   I were putting the food on the table when the man phone. _____
4   Vicky was sail in the sea when she hitted a rock. _____

5 Match the sentences with the pictures.

1 We looked at our map. We had to walk through a forest to get to the campsite.

2 In this picture we were eating the sandwiches which John and David got from the café. We couldn't eat the sausages because they burned black!

3 Last week I went camping with my friends John and David. When we got off the bus it was raining.

4 Our feet were hurting after the long walk and we were tired and hungry when we arrived.

5 It was getting late when we were walking through the forest and it was very dark.

6 This is a picture of me when I was cooking the sausages. I'm not a very good cook.

6 Read and answer 'yes' or 'no'.

1 He went camping with his friends David and John. **yes**

2 It was raining when they got off the bus. _____

3 They had to walk up a hill to get to the campsite. _____

4 The Sun was coming up when they were walking through the forest. _____

5 Their feet were hurting when they arrived at the campsite. _____

6 When he was cooking the sausages, he burned them. _____

7 Read and answer.

Hi Sarah,

This is a funny photo of me at the airport! We were waiting for our plane when I started to feel hungry so I decided to buy an ice cream. There weren't many people waiting to buy one. When I was giving the man the money, someone put their suitcase down on the floor behind me. I didn't see it! I was starting to eat my ice cream when my mum called me to go and catch my plane. I turned quickly and I fell over the suitcase and ... my face went into my ice cream! When I stood up, I had a chocolate ice cream on my nose! My mum thought I looked really funny, so she took the photo! How were your holidays?

See you soon,

Katy

1 What were Katy and her mum doing in the airport? **They were waiting for their plane.**

2 Were there many people waiting to buy an ice cream? _____

3 When did someone put their suitcase down behind her? _____

4 What was she starting to do when her mum called her? _____

5 What did her mum think when she stood up? _____

27

8 Look at the picture. Find the words a–l in the wordsearch.

s	o	o	p	d	r	o	h	r	y
l	e	r	f	n	c	w	e	s	t
e	b	c	e	o	n	t	k	t	g
e	a	h	e	s	r	n	o	s	h
p	c	s	n	k	t	e	n	t	i
i	t	a	t	a	z	y	s	a	l
n	o	e	m	p	n	r	e	t	l
g	r	e	x	p	l	o	r	e	r
b	c	s	q	i	u	g	r	l	a
a	h	t	n	x	s	o	u	t	h
g	r	u	c	k	s	a	c	k	h

9 Write the words. Add the correct letters from Activity 8.

1 camp_____ = to live and sleep outdoors | a |

2 _____ = a bag you can sleep in | |

3 _____ = the opposite of north | |

4 _____ = something you can use to see when it's dark | |

5 _____ = a high place that's lower than a mountain | |

6 _____ = a place where you can sleep | |

10 Write definitions for three more words in Activity 8. Add the correct letters.

_____ | |

_____ | |

_____ | |

11 Look at the code. Write the secret message in your notebook.

> N = north   S = south   E = east   W = west

When – 5E – 4N – 2W – 3S – 2W – 1N – 3E – 2S – 4N – 2W – 3S – 2W – 2N – 5E – 1S –
2W – 2S – 2W – 1E – 2N – 2W – 2N – 1E – 1S – 2E – 1W – 2E – 2S – 1E.

a	warm,	carry	walking	always	are
You	dry	and	jacket	a	should
fruit,	hills,	some	a	you	take
rucksack.	the	a	in	mobile	phone. ➜
➜ When	of	water,	bottle	should	you

28

12 Read the sentences. Draw and write on the map.

 The New Forest is 5 km north of Starton.

The hills are 3 km east of the New Forest.

There's a bridge over the river 5 km west of the New Forest.

2 km south of the hills there's a hotel. Its name is the Happy Inn.

There's a lake 5 km west of Starton. It's called Windymere.

Old Hampton is 2 km north of Windymere.

The campsite is 3 km east of Old Hampton.

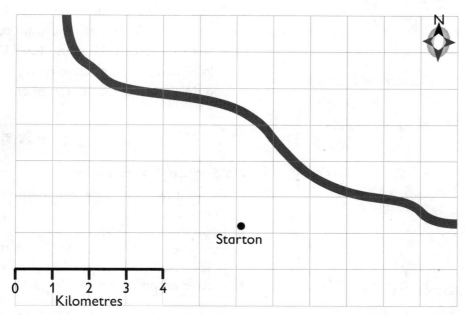

Starton

0   1   2   3   4
Kilometres

13 Now draw these things on the map in Activity 12. Write the directions.

The torch is _____ .

The rucksack is _____ .

The umbrella is _____ .

The suitcase is _____ .

14 Find the letters on the clock.
Write the words.

1   It's quarter to eight. **south** _____
2   It's five past ten. _____
3   It's twenty-five past eight. _____
4   It's quarter past six. _____
5   It's twenty past ten. _____

15 Write times to make four more words in your notebook.

16 Read the words. Cross out the silent letters.

sand~~w~~ich   straight   light   **fire**   farm   **castle**   climb   **wrong**   **half**

Wednesday   corner   should   talking   **knife**   write   **daughter**

17 Write four more words with silent letters. Cross out the silent letters.

hou~~r~~ _____   _____   _____   _____

18 Read and complete.

a weekend	Friday	14 June
family	tent for five	~~website~~

12 Greenfield Close
Kidsbridge
KB6 2B4U
20 March

Sunnyday Campsite
Cornfield Lane
Hillside
Hi De Hi 20

Dear Sir or Madam,
I saw your (1) **website** on the Internet and I'm writing to get some information about your campsite.
  I'd like to come with my (2) _____ and we'd like to stay for (3) _____, from (4) _____ 12 June to Sunday (5) _____ . Please could you tell me if you have a space for these dates?
  We haven't got a tent, so I would also like more information about hiring a (6) _____ . Please could you tell me how much this will cost?
  On your website it says there's a swimming pool near the campsite. Please could you send me a timetable? I would like to know if it opens on Sundays.

Yours faithfully,

Michael Wishful

19 Write a letter to the campsite. Use the information below.

You want to go with your seven friends for a week in August. You want to go from Tuesday to Monday. You'd like information about horse-riding. There's a riding school on the campsite.

Dear Sir or Madam,
I saw your

DIGGORY BONES

20 **Read and answer.**

1 Who was getting out of the car behind them? <u>Richard Tricker.</u> ----------------------

2 Where's the Temple of Quetzalcoatl? ---

3 How far is Mexico City from the hotel? ---

4 Why does the man know about this place? ---

5 What does the long street join? ---

6 Was Diggory expecting to see Iyam there? ---

21 **Put the verbs into the past.**

The story of Mexico City

In about 1325 some young Aztec men (1) <u>were getting</u> (are getting) food for their people when

they (2) ---------------------- (see) an eagle. It (3) ---------------------- (is sitting) on a plant which

(4) ---------------------- (is growing) on a rock in the middle of a lake called Texcoco. They

(5) ---------------------- (think) it (6) ---------------------- (is) a special sign and they

(7) ---------------------- (decide) to build their city there.

    The Aztecs (8) ---------------------- (are) great engineers. They (9) ---------------------- (take)

the water away from the lake to make the island bigger. They (10) ---------------------- (build) canals

so people (11) ---------------------- (can) move around the city by boat, and bridges which they

(12) ---------------------- (take) away at night to protect their city. They (13) ----------------------

(call) their city Tenochtitlan and it (14) ---------------------- (becomes) one of the biggest and most

important cities in the world at that time. The Aztecs (15) ---------------------- (are) very rich because

they (16) ---------------------- (have) land, farms, markets and shops. They (17) ----------------------

(use) the Mayan number system and calendar and they (18) ---------------------- (study) the stars and the

night sky carefully. Like the Ancient Egyptians, they (19) ---------------------- (write) with pictures on

a kind of paper. The name of the Aztec people at the time (20) ---------------------- (is) 'the Mexica'.

? Do you remember?

1 What <u>were</u> ------------- you doing at six o'clock yesterday?

2 I was ----------------- TV.

3 When I go camping, I sleep in a ----------------- in my tent.

4 Marco Polo travelled ----------------- from China to Italy.

5 I can't hear the letter ----------------- in the word 'listen'.

6 Please ----------------- you send me a timetable?

Can do I can talk about explorers using *north*, *south*, *east* and *west*. :(:| :)

I can use the past continuous tense to talk about the past. :(:| :)

I can write a letter asking for information. :(:| :)

1 Find six differences.

A

B

In Picture A, there are two boys and a girl. In Picture B, there are two girls and a boy.

----

2 Read and draw a picture.

This picture is a landscape on a sunny day. The top quarter of the picture is the sky which has a big bright sun in the top left-hand corner. On the other side of the page there are three high mountains which have a little bit of snow on top.

There is a river which comes down from the mountain in the middle and ends in a lake in the bottom right-hand corner of the picture.

There are five tents in a campsite which is to the right of the river. The tents are all different colours and sizes.

On the left of the picture we can see a small hotel. There are some gardens round the hotel and on one side of the hotel there's a car park. There are two cars in the car park.

3 Draw four more things on the picture for your friend to find.

4 Write about one of the pictures from Pupil's Book page 33 in your notebook.

5 Read and choose the right words.

1 The first artists to paint the
  outside world were ...   a Spanish.   b English.   c (Roman.)
2 Landscape painting became popular
  in the ...   a 5th century.   b 18th century.   c 20th century.
3 Artists were trying to copy ...   a nature.   b other artists.   c exams.
4 The French impressionists
  started in the ...   a 1850s.   b 1860s.   c 1870s.
5 The impressionists used ...   a big brush strokes.   b thick lines.   c small spots.
6 Gauguin and Van Gogh used ...   a black and white.   b bright colours.   c dark colours.

6 Read and order the text.

	artists of all time. He was born in 1853 in a small country town in Holland. He started to
	he decided to live in the countryside. He painted the land near the town with bright tones:
	He wanted to paint at night, so he put candles on his hat to see better in the dark. He
	Paris, where he met other painters. He loved the idea of impressionist art so
	Many people didn't understand his work and he only sold one painting in his lifetime. In 1987,
	paint when he was 28. There wasn't much sunlight where he lived, so his first
	painted the cafés with lights at the windows, the Moon over the trees and stars in the night sky.
	paintings were very dark and heavy. He used a lot of black, brown and grey. He went to
	someone bought his famous painting, *Vase with Fifteen Sunflowers*, for £25 million.
1	Vincent Van Gogh was one of the most important impressionists and one of the greatest
	yellow, blue, green, light brown, red and orange. He also painted the people that he loved.

7 Write four questions about Van Gogh.

1 When <u>was he born?</u> _____   3 Who _____ ?
2 Where _____ ?   4 Why _____ ?

8 My project

I did my project   at school ☐   at home ☐.
I worked   alone ☐   with a friend ☐   in a group ☐.
I had   lots of ☐   some ☐   no ☐   problems.
The project was   interesting ☐   OK ☐   boring ☐.
I want to remember: _____
_____

33

Countable and uncountable nouns

Countable nouns	Uncountable nouns
We can count them: bananas, apples ...	We can't count them: water, bread ...
There **aren't enough** chairs.	There **isn't enough** water.
There **are too many** people.	There's **too much** bread.

1 Follow the uncountable food words.

breakfast	water melon	banana	chips	egg	fries	lunch	lime
orange	burger	fruit juice	chocolate	lemonade	soup	lemon	orange juice
bread	carrot	flour	sandwich	mango	pasta	sausage	water
rice	milk	meat	coconut	grape	tea	pea	pepper
vegetable	picnic	apple	dinner	beans	coffee	sugar	salt

How much? →

→ Only a little.

2 Read and match.

1	In some countries there isn't	a	because she felt ill.
2	They couldn't make any bread	b	enough food for everyone to eat.
3	He didn't have many eggs	c	because they didn't have enough flour.
4	We didn't feel well	d	so they decided to give some to their friends.
5	They had too many apples	e	so he bought some more at the supermarket.
6	She didn't eat much at lunchtime	f	because we ate too much ice cream at the party.

☐
1
☐
☐
☐
☐

3 Read and choose the right words.

1 I feel ill because I ate **too many** / (**too much**) chocolate this morning.
2 I can't buy that because I haven't got **enough** / **too many** money.
3 Are there **too many** / **too much** sandwiches?
4 There aren't **enough** / **too much** buses in my town.
5 I like going to the beach when there aren't **too much** / **too many** people.
6 There isn't **enough** / **too much** juice for everyone.

4 Write four sentences in your notebook about your city.

There are too many cars.
There aren't enough parks.

5 Complete the sentences.

| too many | ~~enough~~ | is |
| too much | haven't | enough |

1 There aren't **enough** sandwiches for us.

2 There are _____ people on this bus.

3 Have you got _____ time to help me with the cake, Peter?

4 Oh no! I _____ got enough money!

5 There _____ enough milk for everyone.

6 I think we've got _____ homework this weekend.

6 Complete the conversation. Write a letter (A–F) for each answer.

> A OK. We won't have sausages. I know. Let's have some rice and chicken.
>
> B Let me see … No, I'm sorry. We haven't got enough spaghetti.
>
> C That's a good idea. So it's chicken, rice and a salad.
>
> D Yes, we all like pizza, but there isn't enough flour or enough cheese.
>
> E ~~I don't know. What would you like?~~
>
> F How about some sausages and a salad?

1 What are we going to have for lunch, Dad? `E`

2 Can we have spaghetti, please? It's my favourite. ☐

3 What about pizza then? Can you make us a pizza, please? ☐

4 OK Dad, what ideas have you got? ☐

5 Er, no thanks. I've had too many sausages this week. I had some on Monday and yesterday. ☐

6 That sounds better. Can we have a salad too, please? ☐

Great. Let's start cooking.

7 Write about the picture. Use 'too much', 'too many', 'enough' and the words in the box.

| ~~chair~~ | fork | water | pasta |
| cake | banana | plate | |

There are enough chairs. _____

_____

_____

_____

_____

_____

_____

8 What do you think? Answer the questions.

1 Do you eat enough fruit?

_____

2 Do you eat enough fish?

_____

3 Do you eat too much sugar?

_____

4 Do you eat too many sweets?

_____

5 Do you eat too many chips?

_____

6 Do you drink enough water?

_____

9 Label the photos.

| butter | biscuit | chopsticks | jam | ~~snack~~ | pan | sauce | popcorn |

1 snack _____   2 _____   3 _____   4 _____

5 _____   6 _____   7 _____   8 _____

10 Write the words.

1 We put this on food to make it taste better. It can be hot or cold. sauce _____

2 This is something we eat between meals. _____

3 These pieces of wood or plastic are used for eating. _____

4 This is made from fruit. We can put it on bread. _____

5 We use this to cook in. _____

6 Lots of children like these snacks. They are often round. _____

7 This snack is popular when people go to the cinema. _____

8 You can put this on the bread first when you make sandwiches. _____

11 Write definitions for these words.

1 sandwich _____

_____

2 picnic _____

_____

3 knife _____

_____

12 Read and complete the sentences with 1, 2, 3 or 4 words.

Potato crisps are very popular as a snack all over the world. George Crum invented them in the USA. At the restaurant where he worked, fries were popular. One day someone wasn't happy because the fries were too thick. Crum made them thinner and thinner until finally, he made fries that were too thin to eat with a fork. The man in the restaurant was happy and people around the world started to eat potato crisps. In the USA, crisps are called 'chips' and in Britain, fries are called 'chips'.

1 Potato crisps are a very popular _____ snack all over the world.

2 A man from _____ invented them.

3 He made the first crisps because a man thought his fries _____ .

4 Finally Crum made the crisps _____ _____ with a fork.

5 Fries are called 'chips' _____ .

13 Join the children with their snacks. Write sentences.

Helen   Katy   Michael

Sarah   David   Robert

1   <u>Helen's favourite snack is bread and butter.</u>

2   --

3   --

4   --

5   --

6   --

14 Read the poem. Find the word.

The first letter in 'snack'. I'm hungry, you see. | s |

The second in 'jam'. The fruit's from a tree. | |

The third in 'sausage'. A hot dog to eat. | |

The fourth in 'popcorn'. Salted or sweet. | |

The fifth in 'butter'. I love it on bread. | |

It's something to do with food, I said.

Look at the word and write the letter.

With me, for sure, a dish will taste better.

What am I? ----------------

15 Read and answer 'yes' or 'no'.

Chopsticks

People in Asia use many different things to eat with, for example hands, spoons, forks, knives and chopsticks.

Chopsticks can be big or small. Most Chinese chopsticks are about 25 cm long. For cooking, they also use longer chopsticks, which can be more than 50 cm long. In Japan chopsticks are shorter and they come to a point at one end.

Chopsticks are made of a number of materials, but most are made of wood or plastic. A long time ago they put silver on the end of the chopsticks.

Things you should or shouldn't do when you eat with chopsticks

- Do not move your chopsticks around.
- Do not pick food up by making a hole in it with your chopsticks.
- Do not pull dishes towards you with chopsticks. Use your hands.
- Pull dishes close to you when eating. Put them back after you use them.
- You can lift your dish up to your mouth to eat small pieces of food.

1   Chopsticks are always long. <u>no</u>___

2   They are the same size in Japan and China. _____

3   They are usually made of plastic or wood. _____

4   Use them to make holes. _____

5   Move your chopsticks a lot. _____

6   Pick your bowl up. _____

37

16 Complete the words with 'ph', 'gh', 'f', 'ff' or 'v'. Practise telling the story.

Da **v** id's a __amous __otogra__er. He li__es in a big city and he lo__es ha__ing break__ast in a ca__é which is __ery __riendly. He lea__es home at se__en o'clock e__ery day and he goes there __or a cup o__ his __a__ourite __rench co__ee. Last __riday e__ening, a__ter work, he __oned all his __riends and __amily and in__ited e__eryone to ha__e a lo__ely co__ee there with him. Se__enty of them arri__ed, so there weren't enou__ chairs!

17 Read and order the instructions.

Bread and tomato snack

Ingredients:
- 8 slices of bread
- Olive oil
- 1 piece of garlic
- 3 large tomatoes
- 1 small onion
- Black pepper

What you do:

[ ] Cover each side of the bread with oil. Take the skin off the garlic and cut it in half.

[ ] Then take the skin off the onion and chop the onion into very small pieces. Mix with the tomatoes and a little pepper.

[ ] Rub the garlic over both sides of the bread. Place on a metal tray and cook for 15 minutes.

[ ] When the bread has been cooked for 15 minutes, take it out of the oven. Put some of the tomato mixture onto each piece of bread. Put it back in the oven for another 5 minutes.

[1] Turn the oven on at 200°C.

[ ] While that's cooking, take the skin off the tomatoes and then chop them.

Write it right

A recipe
- A recipe gives instructions so someone can cook something.
- First we include all the food we need. These are the **ingredients**.
- Then we give careful, numbered **instructions** about how to cook the food.

18 Look at the ingredients and the pictures. Write the recipe. Use these words.

| break | heat | mix |
| cut | put | |

1 Break the biscuits into small pieces.
_____
_____
_____
_____
_____
_____

Cold chocolate biscuit cake

Ingredients:

75 g   25 g   1 tbsp   175 g   200 g

Instructions:

1   2   3

4   5   6

38

19 Read and answer.

1 Why will Diggory have to work quickly? <u>They've only got enough food for three days.</u>

2 When will Iyam tell Diggory where the Sun Stone is? _____

3 Where are the secret caves? _____

4 Why was corn important to the Mayas and the Aztecs? _____

5 What did the Aztecs eat with chocolate? _____

6 What else did the Aztecs eat? _____

20 Correct the sentences.

1 Emily didn't ask Iyam enough questions.
   <u>Emily asked Iyam too many questions.</u>

2 There are pictures of sushi on the Sun Stone.
   _____

3 Butter was the most important Aztec food.
   _____

4 The door to the caves is about three kilometres west.
   _____

5 Iyam shouldn't run because the ground is moving.
   _____

6 Diggory asked Emily to get him some chopsticks.
   _____

Do you remember?

1 We've got too <u>many</u> apples.

2 We haven't got _____ milk.

3 I love butter and strawberry _____ on my bread in the morning.

4 People in China often use _____ to eat with.

5 The word 'photographer' has got two _____ sounds.

6 After you mix the tomatoes, _____ the mixture on the bread.

Can do   I can talk about food.

I can use countable and uncountable nouns.

I can write a recipe.

1 Match the words with the definitions.

1 | y | e | a | s | t |

2 | f | r | i | d | g | e |

3 | m | i | c | r | o | - | o | r | g | a | n | i | s | m |

4 | b | a | c | t | e | r | i | a |

5 | m | o | u | l | d |

6 | y | o | g | h | u | r | t |

a   a place where we keep our food cold ☐

b   a bad micro-organism which can
grow on food ☐

c   something we put in bread to make
the mixture grow [1]

d   this is made of milk mixed with a
bacteria ☐

e   a very small living thing ☐

f   these can be good or bad and can
grow on food ☐

2 Now look at the letters in the grey boxes in Activity 1. Find a food word.

----

3 How many words can you find in 'bacteria'?
cat, air, ---

4 Read the letter and write the missing words.

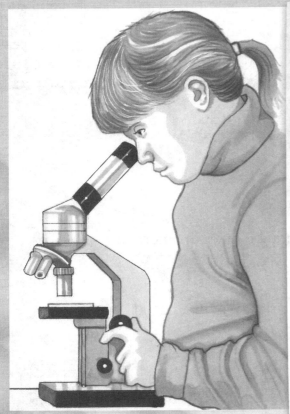

Hi John,

How **(1)** _are_ you? Are you having a good time in Australia? Here in London I'm very busy. This week I've got two exams so I've got to **(2)** ------------------------- Maths and Science. I've also got to do some homework about my favourite job. I want to be a scientist, so I'm **(3)** ------------------------- to write about working in a hospital. My mum's a doctor and she **(4)** ------------------------- with lots of scientists in the hospital. I've got a **(5)** ------------------------- at home and I like looking at small things. I think it's really interesting. **(6)** ------------------------- do you want to do when you're older?

Best wishes,

Katy

5 Choose words from the box to complete the text.

tea	time	clean	milk	UHT	wash	juice	~~bottle~~	bacteria	months

Look at a milk carton or a milk **(1)** _bottle_ . You will see that your milk says it is 'pasteurised' or 'UHT' (in your language). That is because milk can carry bad **(2)** _____ if we drink it directly from the cow. We have to kill the bacteria in the **(3)** _____ to make it safe. Most of the milk we drink today is pasteurised, and there are two different kinds of pasteurisation. These are **(4)** _____ or HTST. UHT stands for 'Ultra Heat Treatment'. This means that for one or two seconds, the milk must be hotter than 135°C. HTST stands for 'High temperature, short **(5)** _____ '. This means that the milk must be at a temperature of 72°C for 15 seconds or more. UHT milk can last for two or three **(6)** _____ before it turns bad, but HTST milk can normally only last for one or two weeks. Do you know other food that is pasteurised?

6 Read again and answer.
1 How many kinds of pasteurisation are there? _There are two._____
2 Is all milk pasteurised? _____
3 What does UHT stand for? _____
4 What temperature must HTST milk be at? _____
5 How long can pasteurised milk last? UHT: _____ HTST: _____

7 Read and match.

1 Keep hot food hot
2 If you have a cut, cover it up
3 Keep cold food cold
4 Wash fruit and vegetables carefully before you eat or cook them
5 Don't cook with pets in the kitchen
6 Keep eggs in the fridge and always cook them before you eat them
7 Keep meat on the bottom shelf of the fridge

because

a animals can carry bacteria.
b bacteria grows above 5°C.
c bacteria grows below 70°C.
d their yellow part (the yolk) can have the bacteria Salmonella.
e cuts can have bad bacteria in them.
f it is colder and meat juices cannot fall onto other food.
g they grow outside where there can be lots of bacteria.

[ ]
[ ]
[1]
[ ]
[ ]
[ ]
[ ]

8 My project

I did my project   at school [ ]   at home [ ] .
I worked   alone [ ]   with a friend [ ]   in a group [ ] .
I had   lots of [ ]   some [ ]   no [ ]   problems.
The project was   interesting [ ]   OK [ ]   boring [ ] .
I want to remember: _____
_____

Review Units 3 and 4

1 Read the story. Choose a word from the box. Write the correct word next to numbers 1–5.

| torch | rucksack | was | too | camp | map | tents | ~~countryside~~ |
| were | enough |

Friendly

Last week's episode of *Friendly* was really funny because there was a school trip to the <u>countryside</u>. The teachers were taking their pupils to a forest to **(1)** _____ . On Friday afternoon when they were waiting for the bus outside the school, Jenny arrived with a really big, heavy suitcase. She said that her **(2)** _____ wasn't very big and she had lots of equipment.

On the way to the campsite Sally sat next to the bus driver because she wanted to watch her drive, look at the directions and follow them on her **(3)** _____ .

When they got to the forest, all five of them had to help Jenny to pull her suitcase across the field to the **(4)** _____ . The ground was too soft and it was really hard work. When they were pulling the suitcase, it fell over again and again.

It was dinner time when they arrived at the campsite and they were dirty, tired and hungry. Jenny was very surprised when she discovered she couldn't use her hairdryer. She couldn't connect it to any electricity in the wall of the tent! Peter was really unhappy because he wanted to cook sausages and beans, but Jim thought a fire was **(5)** _____ dangerous in a forest. Jim took some peanut butter and jam sandwiches out of his rucksack, Sally said she had some popcorn and biscuits and they all laughed when Sue said she was carrying enough cold sushi and chopsticks for everyone! They all agreed that they were eating the strangest camp menu ever!

2 Now choose the best name for the story.

Tick one box.

A drive in the country ☐   Happy camping ☐   Forest fire ☐

3 Which is the odd one out and why?

1 soup   butter   jam   (biscuit)
<u>It's countable.</u> _____

2 chopsticks   fork   torch   spoon
_____

3 best   north   east   south
_____

4 sandwich   sauce   pan   snack
_____

5 tent   cave   sleeping bag   rucksack
_____

6 pasta   bread   cake   cheese
_____

4 Complete the sentences. Count and write the letters.

1 The opposite of east is
   <u>west</u> _____ .   `4`

2 We put _____ with
   peanut butter in sandwiches.   ☐

3 They travelled from Italy
   to China. It was a long
   _____ .   ☐

4 A _____ is like a small
   house. We sleep in it when
   we camp.   ☐

5 A _____ is higher than
   a hill.   ☐

6 They use _____ to eat
   sushi in Japan.   ☐

7 We use a _____ to
   see in the dark when we go
   camping.   ☐

8 I don't like this soup. There's
   _____ much salt in it.   ☐

9 Go from one place to another.
   _____   ☐

10 How _____ butter do
   we need?   ☐

11 A bag which we carry on our
   back is a _____ .   ☐

12 There were too _____
   people at the beach.   ☐

13 'What _____ he doing
   when he fell?' 'He was skiing.'   ☐

14 Something light which we eat
   between meals when we're
   hungry is a _____ .   ☐

15 We only had 50 g of flour. We
   didn't have _____ flour
   to make biscuits.   ☐

5 Write the words in the crossword. Write the message.

1	2	3	4	5	6	7		8	9	10
										t

6 Quiz time!

1 When did Alvin break his arm?
   <u>When he was</u> _____

2 How did impressionist artists paint?
   _____

3 Name an impressionist artist. _____

4 Why couldn't the kids make the cake?
   _____

5 Name two kinds of micro-organism.
   _____

6 How do we make yoghurt?
   _____

7 Write questions for your quiz in your notebook.

5 Under the sea

Present perfect and adverbs

We **still** haven't chosen a project. (= But we have to do it soon.)

The rescue people have been here **since** ten o'clock.
(= When? A point in time: time, date, day, etc.)

It's been here **for** about three hours.
(= How long? How many minutes, hours, days, weeks, etc.)

1 Read and choose the right words.

1 Mr Schwarz has taught me German (for) / since / still three years.
2 It hasn't snowed since **three days / Saturday / two weeks**.
3 I **still / for / since** haven't finished this activity.
4 They **are / have / were** worked here for a year.
5 She hasn't caught a fish **for / since / still** two hours.

2 Complete the sentences with 'for' or 'since'.

1 She's lived in her village since_____ 2008.
2 My little brother has studied English _____ six months.
3 I haven't seen Peter _____ Monday.
4 Mum has had her favourite jacket _____ ten years!
5 I haven't eaten anything _____ nine o'clock.

3 Look at the code (a = ____). Write the secret message.

a	b	c
d	e	f
g	h	i

j	k	l
m	n	o
p	q	r

s	t	u
v	w	x
y	z	

I ' v e _____ _____ _____

4 Write a message in code in your notebook.

5 Find and write four sentences.

liked fishing	three o'clock.	this lesson since
in that flat for	five years.	We've been in
~~He's loved~~	I've	for nine months.
started school.	They've lived	~~Maths since he~~

He's loved Maths since he _____

_____

_____

_____

6 Write sentences about you with 'for' or 'since'.

1 (this room)   I've been in this room for ten minutes. _____
2 (this class)   _____
3 (best friend)   _____
4 (this school)   _____
5 (my house)   _____
6 (English)   _____

7 Use the ideas in Activity 6 to write questions to ask your friend.

1 How long have you been in this room? _____
2 _____
3 _____
4 _____
5 _____
6 _____

8 Read and complete the table.

It's 12 o'clock. There are four children on a bus. Peter was the first boy on the bus. He's been on the bus for ten minutes now, but he's going to get off at the next stop, in two minutes.
David was the last to get on. He got on two minutes ago, but he's going to get off the last.
Helen has been on the bus twice as long as David. She's going to get off at the same stop as Emma.
Emma has been on the bus for the same time as Helen. She's going to get off at the stop after Peter, in four minutes' time.
Helen and Emma are going to get off the bus seven minutes before David.

	Got on the bus?	Going to get off the bus?	How long on the bus in total?
Peter	11.50		
David			
Helen			
Emma			

9 Complete the crossword.

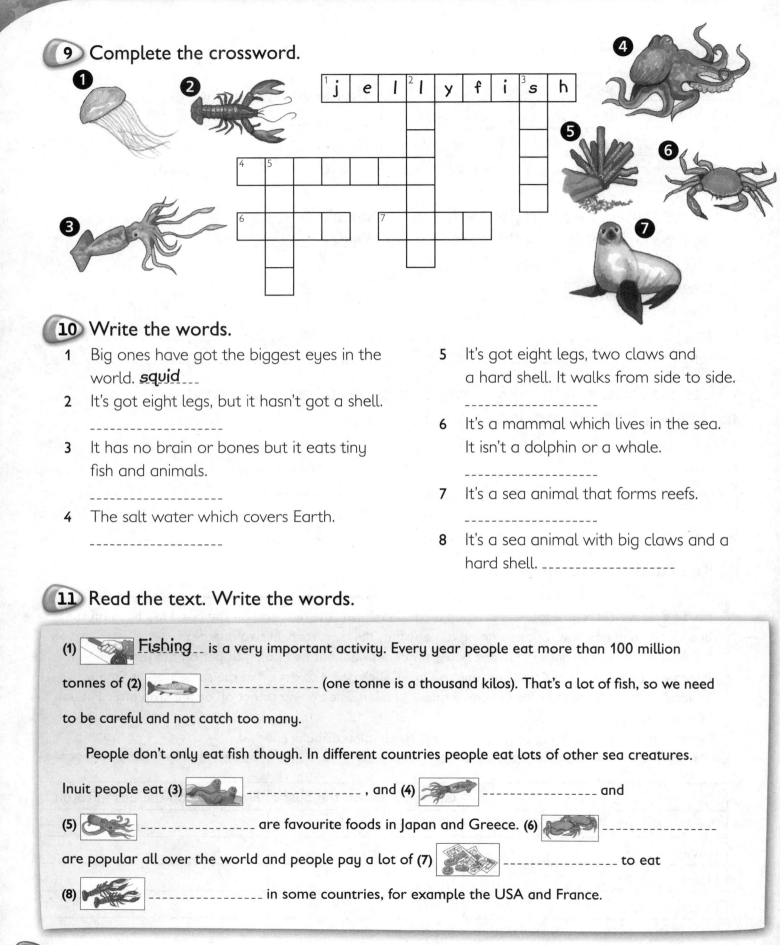

1	j	e	l	l	y	f	i	s	h

10 Write the words.

1 Big ones have got the biggest eyes in the world. **squid**

2 It's got eight legs, but it hasn't got a shell. --------------------

3 It has no brain or bones but it eats tiny fish and animals. --------------------

4 The salt water which covers Earth. --------------------

5 It's got eight legs, two claws and a hard shell. It walks from side to side. --------------------

6 It's a mammal which lives in the sea. It isn't a dolphin or a whale. --------------------

7 It's a sea animal that forms reefs. --------------------

8 It's a sea animal with big claws and a hard shell. --------------------

11 Read the text. Write the words.

(1) **Fishing** is a very important activity. Every year people eat more than 100 million

tonnes of (2) -------------------- (one tonne is a thousand kilos). That's a lot of fish, so we need

to be careful and not catch too many.

People don't only eat fish though. In different countries people eat lots of other sea creatures.

Inuit people eat (3) -------------------- , and (4) -------------------- and

(5) -------------------- are favourite foods in Japan and Greece. (6) --------------------

are popular all over the world and people pay a lot of (7) -------------------- to eat

(8) -------------------- in some countries, for example the USA and France.

46

12 Circle twelve words. Which two are different? Why?

beautiful loud dangerous strong great turtle excited dolphin ice exciting good dirty

_____ and _____ are different. They are _____ .

13 Compare these sea animals. Use adjectives from Activity 12 and your own ideas.

1 jellyfish – seals   _Jellyfish are more dangerous than seals._____
2 coral – an octopus   _____
3 an octopus – a jellyfish _____
4 turtles – lobsters   _____
5 a whale – a squid   _____
6 a shark – a crab   _____

14 Read and colour and write.

Find the octopus which is sitting on the big rock. Colour it purple. Next, look for the squid. There are three. Colour the smallest squid yellow. At the bottom of the picture there's a lot of coral. Colour the coral red. Have you found the lobster? It's in the bottom left corner of the picture. Write 'lobster' above it. At the top of the picture there are some jellyfish. Colour the biggest one blue. There's only one more animal to colour. It's the crab. There are three crabs, but only colour the crab which is inside the big shell. Colour it pink.

15 Read and match.

1 The world's first coral reef   a is the Great Barrier Reef in Australia.   [ ]
2 Storms can   b happened about 500 million years ago.   [1]
3 Scientists have used coral reefs   c they make beautiful white sand.   [ ]
4 When parrot fish eat coral,   d to make a lot of different medicines.   [ ]
5 The biggest reef in the world   e break coral reefs.   [ ]

16 Read the story. Complete the table. Match the pictures with the story.

1 David's lived near the sea since 1995. He's invited his friends Pat and Fred to spend the day with him.

2 Fred's walked to the beach and he's fished since ten o'clock. David's stayed at home to wait for Pat.

3 Pat's texted David to tell him what's happened. She hasn't arrived because her car's stopped outside the village. A kind man's helped her and they've pushed it to a garage. She's decided to leave the car with the mechanic and she's phoned to ask for a taxi.

4 David's talked to Pat. They've agreed that he'll go and fetch her in his car.

5 Now David's closed the front door, he's crossed his garden and he's opened the door of his car. Oh dear! He's dropped his keys and now they're down a hole in the road!

David /ɪd/	Pat /t/		Fred /d/	
invited	walked		lived	

17 Read and complete the factfile.

Seahorses are one of the sea's most interesting animals. They are small fish but their head looks like a horse.

They are different from most other fish because they don't have scales. They have thin skin over the top of bones. There are over 32 kinds of seahorse, which are different sizes and live in different parts of the world. They can live in coral reefs or in water which is not very deep. They swim slowly and can change their colour so that other fish don't eat them. Seahorses eat small fish and krill.

The biggest seahorses can be up to 30 cm long, and the smallest isn't longer than 3 cm from head to tail.

I think they are the most beautiful sea animal.

Write it right

A report
- When you write a report you first need to organise the information.
- Make a factfile with your information. Include interesting facts.
- Give your report a structure: Introduction – Body – Conclusion

18 Make a sea animal factfile in your notebook. Write a report.

FACTFILE – SEAHORSES

Body:	small, head like a horse
Different kinds:	
Where:	
How move:	
Food:	
Interesting fact:	

DIGGORY BONES

19 Read and answer.

1 What has Emily found? <u>She has found a torch.</u>
2 What did Quetzalcoatl get at Teotihuacan? ----------------------------------
3 What kind of shell has Diggory seen? --
4 Why is Iyam like this animal? --
5 Was gold a treasure for the Aztecs? ---
6 What is Richard going to do if they don't help Iyam? ------------------------

20 Write sentences from the story.

1 You / pull / these plants / and / you / open / this cave
<u>You've pulled these plants and you've opened this cave.</u>

2 I / find / a torch
----

3 I / know / about / these caves / 1971
----

4 This / be / the place / their gods / make / the Sun / the Moon / the universe
----

5 There / be / gold here / hundreds of years
----

6 Richard / use / my mobile / follow us

Do you remember?

1 I've been here <u>since</u> ----------- seven o'clock.
2 She's lived in this town --------------- five years.
3 The Pacific ----------------- is the biggest in the world.
4 I think ----------------- reefs are really beautiful.
5 In the words 'walked' and 'asked', the last sound is a ----------------- .
6 Seahorses can change ----------------- .

Can do I can talk about things that have happened using *for* and *since*.

I can talk about sea animals.

I can write a report about sea animals.

49

1 Read and label the pictures.

In the Arctic the biggest land animal, and the top predator on land, is the polar bear. Their favourite food is seals, but they sometimes eat small beluga whales if the whales can't move in the Arctic ice. There are many different kinds of seals in the Arctic and they eat a lot of sea animals. The most important food for seals is fish. Most of the fish eat zooplankton and the zooplankton lives by eating phytoplankton.

seal   zooplankton   phytoplankton   polar bear   ~~fish~~

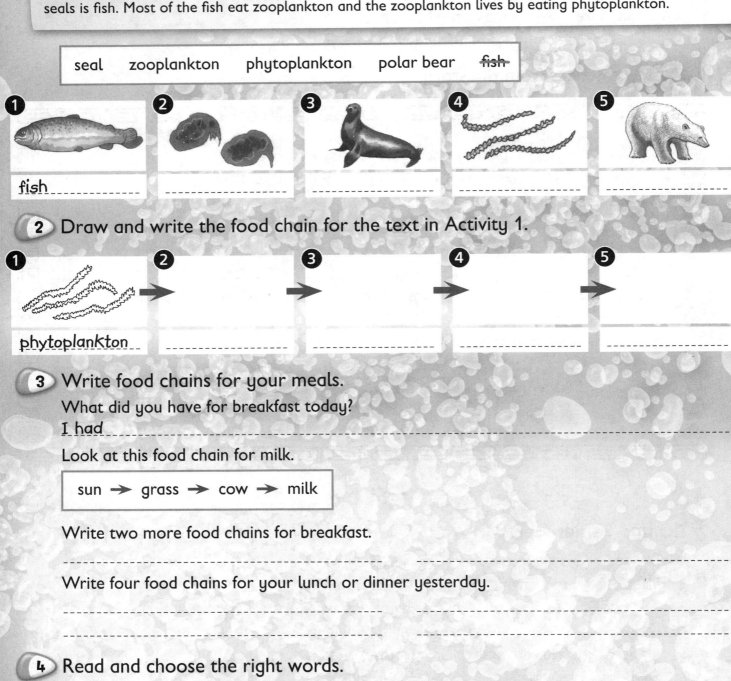

1 fish _____

2 _____

3 _____

4 _____

5 _____

2 Draw and write the food chain for the text in Activity 1.

1 phytoplankton _____

2 _____

3 _____

4 _____

5 _____

3 Write food chains for your meals.

What did you have for breakfast today?
I had _____

Look at this food chain for milk.

sun ➜ grass ➜ cow ➜ milk

Write two more food chains for breakfast.

_____   _____

Write four food chains for your lunch or dinner yesterday.

_____   _____

_____   _____

4 Read and choose the right words.

1 Eagles eat snakes / corn / grass.
2 Snakes eat flour / turtles / lizards.

3 Lizards eat fish / insects / birds.
4 Insects eat fish / plants / mice.

Use your answers to write a land food chain.
plants ➜ _____

5 Choose words from the box to complete the text.

| coral | seahorse | fish | bigger | ~~oceans~~ | thousands | plants | small |

parrot fish

Coral reefs only cover the bottom of 1% of Earth's **(1)** oceans but they are home to 25% of its sea life. There are **(2)** ----------------- of different sea animals. These include **(3)** ----------------- zooplankton and phytoplankton, jellyfish, crabs, octopus and the **(4)** ----------------- turtles and sharks. There are also lots of different **(5)** ----------------- , some with funny names like parrot fish and butterfly fish.

butterfly fish

6 Read and complete the food web.

Remember that the food web hasn't got all the animals, but it helps us to understand that life in the reef is very complicated.

FOOD WEB FACTS

- Zooplankton and jellyfish eat phytoplankton.
- Coral eats zooplankton and phytoplankton. Butterfly fish and jellyfish also eat zooplankton.
- Crabs, parrot fish and butterfly fish eat coral.
- Turtles eat jellyfish.
- Octopus eat parrot fish, butterfly fish and crabs.
- Sharks eat turtles, octopus, butterfly fish, parrot fish and crabs.

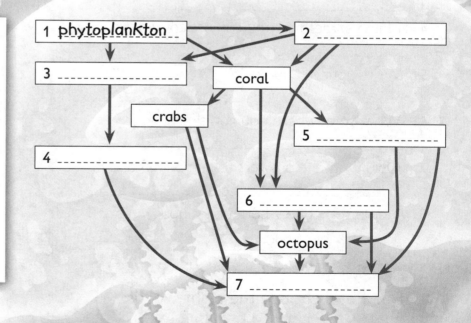

1 phytoplankton

2 -----------------

3 -----------------

coral

crabs

4 -----------------

5 -----------------

6 -----------------

octopus

7 -----------------

7 My project

I did my project   at school ☐   at home ☐.

I worked   alone ☐   with a friend ☐   in a group ☐.

I had   lots of ☐   some ☐   no ☐   problems.

The project was   interesting ☐   OK ☐   boring ☐.

I want to remember: --

LOOK again

some	any	no	every
someone	anyone	no-one	everyone
something	anything	nothing	everything
somewhere	anywhere	nowhere	everywhere

1 Read the test carefully. Follow the instructions.

Reading Test

1 First read ALL the instructions.
2 Write the name of someone you like.
   ----
3 Think of somewhere you like going.
   ----
4 Name something you can use to write.
   ----
5 Write your full name.
   ----
6 Write somewhere you can sleep.
   ----
7 Only write the answers to numbers 5 and 8.
   ----
8 Name someone who teaches you.
   ----

2 Read and choose the right words.

1 I can't see (anything) / something.
2 Is there **everywhere** / **anywhere** I can sit down?
3 I couldn't find my book and I looked **everywhere** / **somewhere**.
4 Can **no-one** / **anyone** give me a pencil, please?
5 Have you got **nothing** / **anything** made of plastic?
6 **Everyone** / **Anyone** stand up, please.

3 Read and complete.

anyone	everywhere
everywhere	inside
~~no-one~~	no-one

A man is watching TV when he hears the door. He opens it but **(1)** no-one is there. He looks **(2)** ------------------ : to the left, to the right, up and finally he looks down and he sees a snail. He's angry so he picks up the snail and throws it really hard. He then goes back **(3)** ------------------ his house.

A month later, the same thing happens. He opens the door but there isn't **(4)** ------------------ there. He looks **(5)** ------------------ , but there's **(6)** ------------------ there. Finally he looks down and sees the snail again. He picks it up, but before he can throw it again, the snail says, 'Why did you do that?'

4 Tell the story in the past. Write it in your notebook.

5 Read and answer.

1 In this sport everyone wears boots. There are 11 players in a team and anyone can kick something which is round. Not everyone can catch the round thing. Only one player can do that.

   a What's the thing which they kick?
      A ball.

   b What's the sport? _ _ _ _ _ _ _ _ _ _ _ _ _ _

   c Who are the people who play this sport?
      _ _ _ _ _ _ _ _ _ _ _ _ _ _

2 In this sport someone puts some long things on their feet and goes to the top of a hill or a mountain. They go down the hill over something which is cold and white.

   a What are the long things which they put on their feet? _ _ _ _ _ _ _ _ _ _ _ _ _ _

   b What are they doing? _ _ _ _ _ _ _ _ _ _ _ _ _ _

   c What's the thing which is cold and white?
      _ _ _ _ _ _ _ _ _ _ _ _ _ _

3 In this sport everyone uses something long to hit something which is very small and round. No-one can kick, catch or throw the small, round thing. They have to hit it into a small hole.

   a What's the sport? _ _ _ _ _ _ _ _ _ _ _ _ _ _

   b Do you play it inside or outside?
      _ _ _ _ _ _ _ _ _ _ _ _ _ _

   c Where is the hole? _ _ _ _ _ _ _ _ _ _ _ _ _ _

6 Write a definition for a sport or a hobby. Use the words from the 'Look again' box on page 52.

_ _
_ _
_ _
_ _
_ _

7 Match the sentences with the pictures.

a ~~Would anyone like to play tennis?~~
b Let's go somewhere different on holiday this year.
c No-one wants to play soccer today.
d There's nowhere for us to play.

8 Read and order the text.

☐ could do it, but No-one did it. Someone was angry, because really it was

☐ do it, but No-one thought that Everyone wasn't going to do it.

☐ In the end Everyone was really angry with Someone when No-one did what Anyone could do.

1 Once upon a time there were four children in a class. Their names

☐ Their teacher asked for some help in the classroom. Everyone thought

☐ that Someone was going to do it. It wasn't difficult, so Anyone

☐ something that Everyone could do. Everyone thought that Anyone could

☐ were No-one, Anyone, Someone and Everyone.

53

9 Label the photos.

1 b e a t b o x
2 _ _ _ _ _ _ _
3 _ _ _ _ _ _ _ _
4 _ _ _ _ _
5 _ _ _ _ _ _ _ _ _ _ _ _ _

10 Follow the free time words.

hobby	does	free running	sewing	playing the piano	baseball
clothes design	to	beatbox	Someone	different	chess
skateboarding	places	table tennis	bored.	goes	skating
mountain biking	things	cooking	interesting	never	reading
board games	skiing	golf	and	is	who

11 Look at the other words in Activity 10. Use them to write a sentence.

Someone _____

_____

12 Read and answer.

When people first started free running, they did it to get from one place to another using the quickest path. They ran and jumped from wall to wall, and down steps. Now they try to do it in the most beautiful way possible.

In Britain, free running became popular in 2003 after someone made a TV programme about it.

Free running has also been on a music video by the pop star Madonna. We can see it in action films and adverts on TV, and there is also a 'Free running' video game.

It is important to remember that it is something which not everyone can do because free runners need to be very strong and fit. It is also difficult and it can be dangerous.

1 When did free running become popular in Britain? In 2003. _____
2 Which pop star used free running in her music video? _____
3 Where else can you see free running? _____
4 Can everyone do free running? _____
5 Why / Why not? _____

13 Find four differences.

A
B

In Picture A, two boys are playing chess. In Picture B, they are girls. ----------

----

----

14 Read the email. Choose the right words and write them on the lines.

Hi Mary,

How are you? Did **(1)** _you_ have a good holiday? **(2)** _____ was great.
I went to a special activity camp and I've started some new hobbies.
(3) _____ was at the camp for five days and **(4)** _____ did something
different every day! The first two days it was raining so we played board
games and I learned to play chess. I also designed some clothes!
On Wednesday they took **(5)** _____ to the hills where we rode amazing
mountain bikes. It was really exciting. Pete taught **(6)** _____ how to
skateboard on Thursday morning so I spent all afternoon skateboarding with
my friends. Friday was **(7)** _____ last day and we did beatbox and rap!
(8) _____ only problem now is that I have too many hobbies!
Emma

1	they	you	us
2	Mine	I	You
3	He	We	I
4	him	we	them
5	we	they	us
6	me	her	you
7	his	me	our
8	I	Me	My

15 Write questions for the answers.

1 _Where did she go?_ ----------------
She went to an activity camp.

2 ----------------------------------
She was there for five days.

3 ----------------------------------
Because it was raining.

4 ----------------------------------
She learned to play chess.

5 ----------------------------------
They rode amazing mountain bikes.

6 ----------------------------------
They did beatbox and rap.

16 Write an email to a friend about your hobbies in your notebook.

17 Join the words where there's a /w/ sound between them.

1 Do I play football well?
2 No, I don't.
3 Who are you?
4 'You're funny.' 'So are you.'
5 You're too old for this.

6 He ran through our garden.
7 He's going to eat something.
8 Go upstairs and clean your teeth!
9 Have you ever been to London?
10 'I'm doing something.' 'So am I.'

18 Read the review and answer.

Yesterday I listened to Bruce Star's new single, 'Happily Happy'. This is the second song from Bruce's new CD 'Bigger', which came into the shops at the start of February. In my opinion this is the best song Bruce has written since he left his old band 'The Starlets'. I love the chorus, when he repeats 'Happily Happy', and I think he sings the song beautifully. I also like the drums, which are strong and loud. The only thing I don't like much is the sound of the guitar. I think it sounds too fast. I prefer it when he plays the guitar more slowly.

◄ **Write it right**

Expressing opinions
In my opinion ...
I like / love ...
I think / don't think ...
I prefer ...

1 What's the song called? 'Happily Happy'. _____
2 Who sang it? _____
3 What album is it from? _____
4 What does the writer like most about it? _____
5 What else does she like? _____
6 What doesn't she like and why? _____

19 Think of your favourite song. Answer the questions in your notebook.

• What's the song called?   • What album is it from?   • What else do you like?
• Who sang it?   • What do you like most?   • Is there anything you don't like? Why?

20 Now write a review.

I'm going to review _____
_____
_____
_____
_____
_____

21 Read and answer.

1 Where are they going to go?
   Somewhere nearer the sea.

2 What will take Iyam to a cave of gold?
   ----

3 Are Kukulcan and Quetzalcoatl the same?
   ----

4 What's Kukulcan's temple called?
   ----

5 What did the Mayas do before their ball game?
   ----

6 In what months can you see the snake on the stairs?
   ----

22 Look at the code. Write the secret message in your notebook.

N = north	S = south	E = east	W = west

Tlachtli – 5E – 4S – 2W – 3N – 3W – 3S – 4E – 4N – 1S – 3W – 3S – 2N – 4E – 2W – 2N – 1W – 4S – 1N – 2W – 5E – 2N – 3W – 1S – 2W – 4E – 1S – 1W – 2W – 3N.

Tlachtli	walls.	ball	rubber	played.	was
which	had	stone	game	They	of
up	pass	high	heavy	in	a
circle	the	a	of	one	made
Mayan	to	through	ball	men	a

? Do you remember?

1 Is there **anywhere**......... I can sit down?
2 I've looked ------------------- but I can't find my pen.
3 ------------------- is a very old board game.
4 Music and rhythm which you make with your mouth is called ------------------- .
5 In the question 'Who is he?', we can hear a ------------------- sound between 'Who' and 'is'.
6 In my ------------------- , pop music is the best kind of music.

Can do   I can use words to talk about something, anything, nothing and everything.

I can talk about different hobbies.

I can write a song review.

1 Do the music questionnaire.

1 Do you like opera? ---
2 Do you like rock music? --
3 How often do you listen to music? --
4 Who's your favourite singer? ---
5 Which is your favourite group? ---
6 How do you listen to music? (radio, MP3, CDs, etc.) --------------------------
7 Do you buy music from shops? ---
8 Do you download music from the Internet? -------------------------------------

2 Ask someone else the questions. Write about your answers in your notebook.

My dad likes opera, but I don't. We both --------------------------------------

3 Read and choose the best title for each paragraph.

Break dancing	~~The world of hip hop~~	How hip hop began	Street art

1 The world of hip hop --
Rap and beatbox are both different kinds of the music that we call hip hop. The word 'hip hop' can describe music or it can describe other parts of life. These include graffiti art and dancing.

2 --
Hip hop music started in the 1970s, when DJs started to play and repeat the rhythmic parts of some records for people to dance to. In between songs the DJs started to talk, to tell people to dance and to have a good time. This talking changed into rap as the DJs used rhyme and rhythm, as we have in the rap music of today. Now rappers often rap to the sound of someone doing beatbox.

3 --
Graffiti is a kind of art that we see on the streets. At first graffiti artists painted on walls or trains because they were angry and wanted people to see their different kind of painting. Today some graffiti artists have their paintings in galleries (art museums) and books, and they sell their paintings for a lot of money.

4 --
With the start of hip hop music, a different kind of dancing also started. Sometimes this is called break dancing, or b-boying. This kind of dancing is very athletic, with a lot of quick movements, and break dancers often dance in the street or in playgrounds.

4 Read again and complete the sentences with 1, 2, 3 or 4 words.

1 Hip hop includes other types of music, for example **rap and beatbox.** -------------
2 Hip hop can describe music and ---.
3 The first hip hop music started --.
4 The DJs used ---------------------------------- when they talked and this was the first rap music.
5 Today you can buy a graffiti painting for --------------------------------------
6 Break dancing is --- b-boying.

5 Read and order the text.

☐	trumpet, with no words. When he finished playing in the 1960s, some writers described
☐	family didn't have much money so after he left school at the age of 11, he sang with
☐	the way he played the melodies. In some songs his singing sounds like a
1	Louis Armstrong was one of the world's most famous jazz musicians. He was a trumpet
☐	and sang with all the world's best musicians. He was famous for his improvisation and
☐	player and a jazz singer. Louis was born in 1901 in New Orleans in the USA. His
☐	him as the most important American musician of the 20th century.
☐	14 he was working in his first band. During his life Armstrong played the trumpet
☐	a group of boys to get money. He started playing the trumpet at the same age and at

6 Read again and answer.

1 What was Louis's surname? **Armstrong.**_____

2 When was he born? _____

3 Where was he born? _____

4 How old was he when he left school? _____

5 When did he start playing the trumpet? _____

6 What was he famous for? _____
_____

7 Look at this factfile for Biz Markie. Write a short biography.

FACTFILE

Name: Marcel Hall

Born: 8 April, 1964, in New York

School: Long Island High School

First job: DJ in New York clubs – new name Biz Markie

First record: 1985 single 'Def Fresh Crew'

Musical style: hip hop, rap and beatbox

Other jobs: actor in the film *Meteor Man*

Biz Markie's real name _____
_____
_____
_____
_____
_____
_____
_____
_____
_____
_____
_____
_____

8 My project

I did my project   at school ☐   at home ☐.

I worked   alone ☐   with a friend ☐   in a group ☐.

I had   lots of ☐   some ☐   no ☐   problems.

The project was   interesting ☐   OK ☐   boring ☐.

I want to remember: _____
_____

Review Units 5 and 6

1 Read the story. Choose a word from the box. Write the correct word next to numbers 1–5.

ridden	someone	~~hobbies~~	chess	cook	nowhere	dangerous
anything	squid	ocean				

Friendly

In today's episode the friends are talking about the <u>hobbies</u> that they do in their free time. Jim's started free running and is really excited about it. He says he got the idea when he saw the film *The Harder They Run* and the actor, Bruce Willis, had to run through a city centre. Sally says she loves action films and that there are special actors who do all the tricks. Her favourite is Max Limit. Max has driven cars at over 200 kilometres an hour, he's flown lots of different planes and he's **(1)** _____ motorbikes, horses and elephants. Jenny doesn't find any of this exciting and she tells Jim that she thinks his new hobby is strange and too **(2)** _____ .

Sue's hobby isn't dangerous, but once when she was painting a small waterfall in the countryside, she fell into the river, which was moving very fast, and **(3)** _____ had to pull her out.

Peter loves trying new things to eat. He says he'll try anything. He's eaten octopus and **(4)** _____ before, but on his last holiday in Japan, he and his parents ate blowfish. This fish is very, very poisonous and someone has to prepare and cook it very well or you can die when you eat it.

Jenny tries to remember the most dangerous thing she's ever done. Jim laughs because he can't believe she's ever done **(5)** _____ dangerous. Jenny says that once she ate one of Sue's dishes and everyone knows that she's a terrible cook!

2 Now choose the best name for the story.
Tick one box.

Living dangerously ☐   Hard actors ☐   Eating seafood ☐

3 Which is the odd one out and why?

1 golf (badminton) soccer tennis
<u>You don't play it with a ball.</u>

2 seen ridden walked thought
_____

3 baseball volleyball soccer
basketball
_____

4 crab jellyfish lobster turtle
_____

5 skates skis chess skateboards
_____

6 laughed arrived remembered
turned
_____

4 Complete the sentences. Count and write the letters.

1 'How many fish has that dolphin __eaten__ ?' 'Six.' `5`

2 In _____ people run and jump through a city centre. ☐

3 A sea animal without claws which has got eight legs. It isn't a squid. _____ ☐

4 _____ is a black and white board game. ☐

5 An _____ is usually bigger than seas, rivers and lakes. ☐

6 'Is there _____ in the café?' 'No, everyone's gone.' ☐

7 A _____ is something hard on the outside of an animal's body. A turtle's got one. ☐

8 We stand on a _____ to go fast in parks. ☐

9 A _____ is a round animal with eight legs and two arms with claws. ☐

10 He's been a footballer _____ 2005. ☐

11 _____ looks like a little forest but it's lots of sea animals. ☐

12 A _____ is in the same family as dolphins and seals, but it's much bigger. ☐

13 A bat is _____ which we use to hit a ball. ☐

14 'How long have you _____ your mountain bike?' 'A year.' ☐

15 He's been a photographer _____ nine years. ☐

5 Write the words in the crossword. Write the message.

e a t e n

1 2 3 3   4 5 6 3   1 7 8

n

6 Quiz time!

1 What were the people rescuing on the beach? __They were__ _____

2 Why are plants called 'producers'? _____

3 What is a top predator? _____ _____

4 What game did the kids start to play in their classroom? _____

5 What is the music behind the tune? _____

6 How old is opera? _____

7 Write questions for your quiz in your notebook.

7 Dress sense

Possibility

I think it **may** look better with a jacket.   I **might buy** a new jacket.

I **might not** need a jacket.

1 Write the clothes words in alphabetical order.

trousers	sweater	jacket	glasses	dress	watch	~~coat~~	skirt
T-shirt	hat	jeans	shirt	handbag	shoes	scarf	socks

coat,_____

_____

_____

_____

2 Read and choose the right words.

1   He (may buy) / may buys / may to buy a new jacket.
2   She **mights wear** / **might wears** / **might wear** her skirt.
3   It **not might** / **might not** / **isn't might** be cold.
4   You **may prefer** / **mays prefer** / **may prefers** salad with your pizza.
5   They **can't might** / **might not** / **don't might** win this afternoon's game.
6   You **might** / **must** / **can** need a scarf because I think it's cold outside!

3 Write about your clothes.

1   My trousers are made of _____.
2   My jacket is made of _____.
3   My shoes _____.
4   Tomorrow I might wear _____ because _____.
5   At the weekend I might wear _____ because _____.

4 Complete the sentences.

go	visit	~~wear~~	get	get up	watch

1   He might **wear** a jacket this afternoon because it's cold.
2   She might _____ TV after lunch.
3   They might _____ us today.
4   You might not _____ your present until Sunday.
5   I may not _____ shopping tomorrow.
6   We may _____ early on Saturday.

62

5 What do you think it is? Use 'may'.

1 <u>It may be a</u>   2 _____   3 _____   4 _____

_____   _____   _____   _____

6 Look at the picture. Read and answer 'yes' or 'no'.

1 They might have a picnic. **yes**_____
2 She might be lost. _____
3 He may want to catch a bus home. _____
4 She might not be happy. _____
5 It might rain. _____
6 They might need coats. _____

7 Correct the sentences.

1 They mights wear their jeans. <u>They might wear their jeans.</u>_____
2 She does might take a jacket. _____
3 I don't might put on my sweater. _____
4 Peter may plays football tomorrow. _____
5 I might not to wear my black shoes. _____
6 They mays wear their new jackets. _____

8 Find and write five sentences.

Susan	might put	is green	coats and scarves.
Our school	took	of	and red.
Richard	uniform	on their	plastic.
My schoolbag's	wore her	blue spotted	with him.
The children	made	a jacket	belt.

1 <u>Susan wore her blue spotted belt.</u>_____
2 _____
3 _____
4 _____
5 _____

9 Find two words for each group of letters. One is a clothes word.

1 ti- <u>tights</u>, <u>tigers</u>
2 sh- _____, _____
3 po- _____, _____
4 gl- _____, _____
5 u-   _____, _____
6 bu- _____, _____

mbrella   oves   ~~ghts~~   ue
gly   tter
orts   ~~gers~~
opping   tato   cket   tton

10 Label the photos with words from Activity 9.

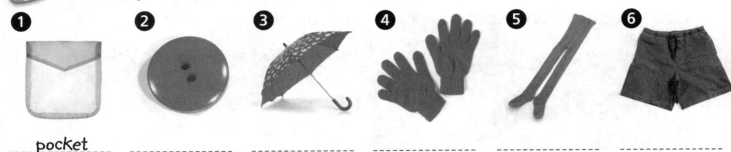

1 ___<u>pocket</u>___   2 _____   3 _____   4 _____   5 _____   6 _____

11 Read and complete the sentences with 1, 2, 3 or 4 words.

Last Saturday Jane went shopping with her Aunt Helen to buy some new clothes. They went to three different clothes shops. The first shop was called Legs Eleven and they had lots of tights. Jane chose some grey and green ones.

Next they went to look for some shorts. They found lots in a shop called 4 Fashion. Jane didn't know which ones to choose, so her aunt helped her. She got a lovely blue pair made of cotton, with big pockets.

In the last clothes shop they bought a beautiful red coat. She didn't buy any new shoes because she's got three pairs at home. When they were coming home, it started to rain so they bought two umbrellas from a small shop. They caught the bus home because they didn't want to get wet.

1 Jane went to the shops with <u>her Aunt Helen.</u>_____
2 Legs Eleven was _____ shop which they went into.
3 Jane's new tights are _____ .
4 Aunt Helen helped Jane _____ some shorts.
5 Jane's new blue _____ cotton and they have big pockets.
6 She didn't need _____ because she's got three pairs.
7 They bought _____ in the last clothes shop.
8 They went home on _____ because it was raining.

12 Read and complete the circle with names and clothes words.

Three girls and two boys are sitting round a table. Richard is sitting between two girls. The girl on his left is called Emma.

The girl on William's left is called Betty.

The girl between Richard and Sarah is wearing a striped T-shirt and a skirt. She has a beautiful gold ring.

The boy with the shorts is wearing a belt. He's also wearing a shirt and a new jacket.

The girl with the scarf isn't wearing a skirt. She's wearing some trousers and a sweater which is made of cotton.

The girl on the right of Richard has got some plastic earrings on. She's also wearing a striped sweater, a skirt and tights.

The other boy is cold so he's wearing some gloves. His sweater is striped and he's also wearing trousers.

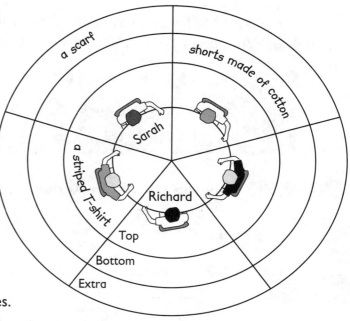

13 Draw a piece of clothing and write about it.

These are my favourite long shorts. They're very, very big so I wear them with a belt. They're dark brown and they've got big pockets on the legs above the knees. My mum hates them, but I love them!

14 Describe the picture.

1 No-one <u>is playing chess.</u>

2 Nothing _____
   _____ .

3 No-one _____
   _____ .

4 Everyone _____
   _____ .

15 Match the sentences with the pictures. Practise saying the sentences with feeling.

a Pizza! My favourite meal!   b What a goal!   c We've lost again!
d What can I do now?   e I'll get your cat!   f Who's there outside the door?

 b

16 Write how the people in Activity 15 are feeling. Use these words.

unhappy   ~~excited~~   bored   afraid   brave   happy

1 He's feeling excited. _____
2 She_____ .
3 He_____ .
4 She_____ .
5 They_____ .
6 She_____ .

17 Look at the pictures. Read and tick (✓) the correct picture.

There are two people in the picture: a man and a woman. The man is taller than the woman, but she's got longer hair. The man's got dark, curly hair and a small beard, but he hasn't got a moustache. He's wearing a long coat over the top of a pair of black trousers and a shirt. He's got black shoes on. He looks like a detective. He's standing next to a woman who's got long, curly, blonde hair. She's got big eyes and a long, thin nose. She's smiling. She's wearing jeans, a short jacket and sports shoes. She looks like a rock star.

> **Write it right**
>
> **Describing people**
> Describe their face and body.
> → He's got a big nose and long, brown, curly hair.
>
> Describe their clothes.
> → She's wearing a beautiful, long, blue, cotton skirt.
>
> Describe what they look like.
> → He looks like an angry chef.

18 Now write a description in your notebook of one of the other pictures. Can your friend guess which picture it is?

19 Read and answer.

1 What did Aztec braves wear? _They wore birds' feathers and animal fur._

2 How did everyone feel when they saw them? _____

3 What did the Mayas do in the round building? _____

4 Why do they have to move fast? _____

5 When do the bowls work like mirrors? _____

6 At what time is the Sun at its highest? _____

20 Put the verbs into the past simple.

The Aztecs (1) _were_ (are) very rich. They (2) _____ (have) fields and water to grow plants for food and materials. They also (3) _____ (have) lots of stone for building, and gold and silver. Like the Mayas, they (4) _____ (get) the liquid from rubber trees and (5) _____ (use) that, too. They (6) _____ (make) balls for their famous ball game and (7) _____ (use) it to clean their teeth after meals. They (8) _____ (invent) the first chewing gum!

Rich Aztec people (9) _____ (wear) more clothes than poor people, and their clothes (10) _____ (are) made from different cloth. Poor people (11) _____ (can't) wear cotton. Women and girls (12) _____ (make) most of their cloth from the 'century plant' and (13) _____ (use) bright colours and designs to decorate it. They (14) _____ (make) shoes from rubber, but if they (15) _____ (have) to go into a temple or see the king, they (16) _____ (can't) wear anything on their feet. When they (17) _____ (dance), they (18) _____ (wear) belts with sea shells to make music as they (19) _____ (move). They sometimes (20) _____ (wear) feathers and animal fur, too. Aztec braves (21) _____ (paint) their faces to look horrible and to make people afraid of them. Married women (22) _____ (put) their hair up on top of their heads. Corn (23) _____ (is) their most important food, but they also (24) _____ (eat) a lot of vegetables. They (25) _____ (don't eat) a lot of meat, but they sometimes (26) _____ (eat) insects and lizards.

Do you remember?

1 It might _rain_ later so I'm going to take an umbrella.

2 I need to study because we _____ have a Maths test tomorrow, but I'm not sure.

3 I've got a new _____ so my trousers don't fall down.

4 When it's cold I wear _____ on my hands.

5 My little brother didn't like the film because he was _____ of the monster.

6 That man with the long coat looks _____ a detective.

Can do
I can talk about possibility using *may* and *might*.
I can talk about clothes.
I can write a description of someone and their clothes.

1 Read and order the text.

Who first sewed clothes?

thread   needle   loom   cloth

[ ] these longer threads on machines called looms to make big pieces of cloth. This

[ ] make clothes about 15,000 BC. They used needles made of bone or wood. The

[ ] put a piece of thread through a hole in one end

[1] Archaeologists think that people began sewing animal skins together to

[ ] basic design of the needle hasn't changed since it was first invented. We

[ ] and then pull it through the pieces of material to join them.

[ ] is very similar to what we use today to make our clothes.

[ ] People later invented ways to make threads longer. They used

2 Look at the code. Write the secret message.

26	25	24	23	22	21	20	19	18	17	16	15	14	13	12	11	10	9	8	7	6	5	4	3	2	1
A	B	C	D	E	F	G	H	I	J	K	L	M	N	O	P	Q	R	S	T	U	V	W	X	Y	Z

23–12 2–12–6 16–13–12–4 4–19–22–9–22 17–22–26–13–8 24–12–14–22 21–9–12–14?
D o   o   y o u   _ _ _ _   _ _ _ _ _   _ _ _ _ _   _ _ _ _   _ _ _ _?

11–22–12–11–15–22 21–18–9–8–7 8–7–26–9–7–22–23 4–22–26–9–18–13–20 7–19–22–14
_ _ _ _ _ _   _ _ _ _ _   _ _ _ _ _ _ _   _ _ _ _ _ _ _   _ _ _

21–12–9 4–12–9–16 25–22–24–26–6–8–22 7–19–22–2 26–9–22 14–26–23–22 12–21
_ _ _   _ _ _ _   _ _ _ _ _ _ _   _ _ _ _   _ _ _   _ _ _ _   _ _

8–7–9–12–13–20 24–15–12–7–19 24–26–15–15–22–23 23–22–13–18–14. 13–12–4 4–22
_ _ _ _ _ _   _ _ _ _ _ ,   _ _ _ _ _ _ _   _ _ _ _ _ .   _ _ _   _ _

26–15–15 4–22–26–9 7–19–22–14, 25–6–7 13–12–7 12–21–7–22–13 26–7 4–12–9–16!
_ _ _   _ _ _ _   _ _ _ _ ,   _ _ _   _ _ _   _ _ _ _ _ _   _ _   _ _ _ _!

3 Use the code to write a question for your friend to read.

_____

_____

4 Use the code to answer your friend's question.

_____

_____

5 Label the picture.

belt	gloves	jacket
scarf	pocket	helmet
trousers	boots	

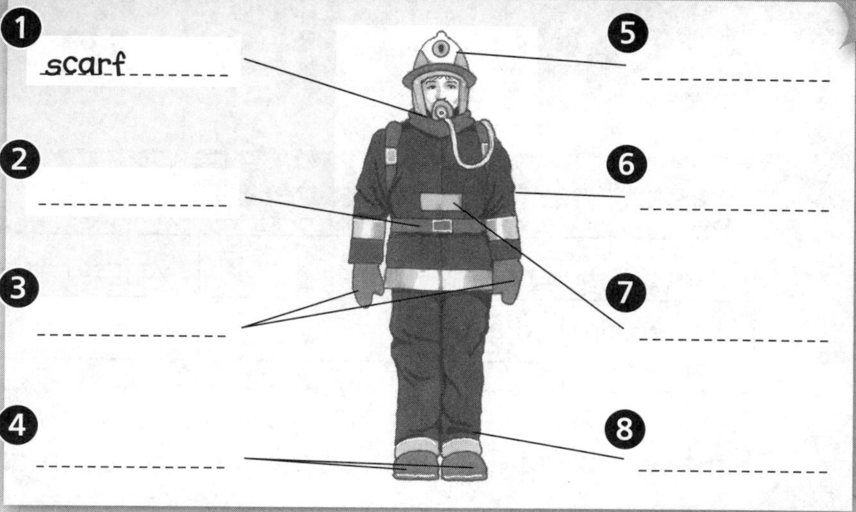

1 scarf
2 _____
3 _____
4 _____
5 _____
6 _____
7 _____
8 _____

6 Write about the firefighter's uniform. Use the text on Pupil's Book page 69 to help you.

| leather | cotton | plastic | metal | rubber |

The gloves are made of _____
_____

7 Label the activities and sports. Write about two of the uniforms.

1 dancing
2 _____ 
3 _____ 
4 _____ 
5 _____

8 My project

I did my project   at school ☐   at home ☐.

I worked   alone ☐   with a friend ☐   in a group ☐.

I had   lots of ☐   some ☐   no ☐   problems.

The project was   interesting ☐   OK ☐   boring ☐.

I want to remember: _____
_____

69

Present perfect and adverbs

Have you finished **yet**?	I've **just** finished this book.
I haven't finished **yet**.	I've **already** finished my project.

1 Find two irregular past participles for each group of letters.

1 b- _been_ , _begun_
2 m- _____ , _____
3 dr- _____ , _____
4 t- _____ , _____
5 th- _____ , _____
6 br- _____ , _____

7 sp- _____ , _____
8 l- _____ , _____
9 c- _____ , _____
10 st- _____ , _____
11 r- _____ , _____
12 go- _____ , _____

aken   awn   ost   ne   oken

aught   ome   ood   ought   eant   ent   ~~een~~   eft

olen   aught   rown   idden

un   oken   t   ought   ~~egun~~   et   iven

2 Complete the sentences with verbs from Activity 1.

1 He's r_idden_ his bike for two hours.
2 They've just g_____ out.
3 This is the third time I've b_____ to read this book!

4 She hasn't s_____ all her money yet.
5 Our cat still hasn't c_____ home.
6 They've just d_____ a picture.

3 Look at the picture. Write sentences.

Come on! Time for breakfast!

1 (get up) _He's already got up._
2 (tidy his room) _He hasn't tidied his room yet._
3 (make his bed) _____
4 (put on his shoes) _____
5 (have breakfast) _____
6 (put on his trousers) _____

4 Write sentences about you today. Use 'already', 'yet' or 'just'.

1 (have lunch) _I've already had lunch. / I haven't had lunch yet. / I've just had lunch._
2 (read something) _____
3 (do some of my homework) _____
4 (listen to music) _____

5 Tick (✓) two more correct sentences. Correct two more sentences.

1 'Tidy your room!' 'I've already tidied it!' ✓ _____
2 He is done his homework already.   He's already done his homework. _____
3 Has he been to Australia?   _____
4 I live here for ten years.   _____
5 They's seen that film already.   _____
6 She's studied English for three years. _____

6 What have they just done?

1 He 's just tidied his room.

2 She _____ .

3 They _____ .

4 She _____ .

5 We _____ .

6 He _____ .

7 Look at the Hirds' plans. Read and answer 'Yes, they have' or 'No, they haven't'.

HOLIDAY!		morning	afternoon
Monday	Cambridge	see the University	play in a park
Tuesday	Nottingham	see the Castle	walk in Sherwood Forest
Wednesday	Liverpool	cross the River Mersey	go shopping
Thursday	York	walk on the Roman walls	visit the Viking Museum
Friday	London	visit the Science Museum	see Big Ben

Now it is Wednesday lunchtime.

1 The Hirds haven't been to Cambridge yet.   Yes, they have. _____
2 They have already seen Nottingham Castle.   _____
3 They have already been shopping in Liverpool. _____
4 They haven't visited the Science Museum yet. _____
5 They've already walked in Sherwood Forest.   _____
6 They haven't played in a park in Cambridge yet. _____

8 Label the car stickers with nationalities. Use the letters in the box.

E   BR

a a a a a c c d
e e e e e e g h
h i i i i k l m n
n n n n n o p r
r r r r s s t u u x
z B F G G I M P s

IND   F

1 Spanish   2 _____   5 _____   6 _____

GR   P

3 _____   4 _____

D   MEX

7 _____   8 _____

9 What countries are these web pages from?

www.mundocrianças.br   1 Brazil _____

www.kinderhere.de   2 _____

www.niñolandia.es   3 _____

www.mondenfant.fr   4 _____

www.kidsofindia.in   5 _____

www.sunfun4kids.gr   6 _____

www.4crianças.pt   7 _____

www.mundoniños.mx   8 _____

10 Read and answer.

Did you know that there are 195 countries in the world? Each of them has a capital city. Some of them even have more than one capital and South Africa has three capitals! Some capitals aren't difficult to learn. For example, it's easy to remember that Mexico City is the capital of Mexico or that Brasilia is the capital of Brazil. We know the names of other capitals because we hear about them in History lessons, the news or sporting events.

You might know that the capital of Spain is Madrid and the capital of Greece is Athens. You may even know that the German capital is Berlin or that the Portuguese capital is Lisbon, but did you know that the Indian capital is New Delhi? Some capitals surprise us because they aren't the biggest city in the country. Did you know that the capital of Australia isn't Sydney? No, it's Canberra, and the capital of the USA isn't New York. It's Washington D.C.

1 Which is the Mexican capital? Mexico City. _____
2 Which is the capital of India? _____
3 Where is Canberra the capital of? _____
4 What's the name of the Greek capital? _____
5 Which is the Spanish capital? _____
6 What's the capital of Portugal? _____
7 Where is Washington D.C. the capital of? _____
8 Which is the Brazilian capital? _____

11 Complete the words with the groups of letters in the box. Use each group for only one pair of words.

sh	~~me~~	any	ey	co	al	try	ch	tal	th

1 Ro…   **me**__ …tal   Yes   (No)
2 Turk…   _____ …es   Yes   No
3 coun…   _____ …ing   Yes   No
4 Germ…   _____ …where   Yes   No
5 Fren…   _____ …opsticks   Yes   No

6 Portug… _____ …ready   Yes   No
7 capi…   _____ …lest   Yes   No
8 Engli…   _____ …orts   Yes   No
9 nor…   _____ …rown   Yes   No
10 Mexi…   _____ …mb   Yes   No

12 Say the pairs of words in Activity 11. Do the letters sound the same in both words? Circle 'Yes' or 'No'.

(Rome … metal)

13 Ask and answer. Write your friend's answers.

1 Have you ever eaten Spanish food?   _____   What was it? _____
2 Have you ever eaten Mexican food?   _____   What was it? _____
3 Have you ever eaten Indian food?   _____   What was it? _____
4 Have you ever eaten Portuguese food?   _____   What was it? _____
5 Have you ever eaten Italian food?   _____   What was it? _____
6 Have you ever eaten Greek food?   _____   What was it? _____
7 Have you ever eaten _____ food?   _____   What was it? _____
8 Have you ever eaten _____ food?   _____   What was it? _____

14 Write a report about international food that you and your friend have eaten.

We haven't eaten Greek food, but I have eaten Portuguese food. I can't remember the word, but it was fish with tomatoes. Igor has eaten Mexican food. He had

_____
_____
_____
_____
_____
_____
_____
_____

15 Follow the words with the 'th' sound in 'think' from 'north' to 'south'.

north —	Earth	this	those	farther	than	mother
grandmother	think	them	photograph	everything	throw	fourth
their	bath	feather	grandfather	thirsty	they	eighth
brother	theatre	there	other	thief	the	through
weather	thousand	clothes	nothing	both	that	thrown
these	thanks	month	Thursday	father	another	south

16 Write these words in order of size from the biggest to the smallest.

city   continent   country   Earth   street   our solar system
town   ~~the universe~~   village

the universe, _____

_____

17 Write five continents, five countries and five capital cities.

Continents: Australia, _____

Countries: _____

Capital cities: _____

18 Read and complete Robert's form.

Woman: How can I help you?

Robert: I'd like to go on your Summer English Course in England.

Woman: Fine, now I need some information to put on the form. First, your name and surname, please.

Robert: Robert Schmidt.

Woman: OK, and when were you born?

Robert: On 15 June 1996.

Woman: Where are you from?

Robert: I'm from Germany.

Woman: And your address, please?

Robert: I live at 35 Bear Street, Berlin.

Woman: What's the postcode?

Robert: I think it's 10117.

Woman: Good, and finally what's your telephone number?

Robert: Err, 689-730241.

Write it right

Completing a form
- Read the headings carefully.
- Does the form want you to use CAPITAL letters?
- Do you have to circle or tick anything?

Please use CAPITAL letters.

Name: ROBERT _____

Surname: _____

Course (please circle): Music / Art / English / Sport

Date of birth: _____

Country of birth: _____

Nationality: _____

Address: _____

Postcode: _____

Telephone number: _____

19 Read and answer.

1 What's Iyam just done? **He's just pushed the corn symbol.**

2 How long has the museum at Balankanche been open? _____

3 How did the Mayas water their fields? _____

4 How long have Interpol wanted Iyam and Richard Tricker? _____

5 What are Sir Doug Bones and Diggory going to do with the Sun Stone? _____

6 What did Emily's grandfather use to follow them? _____

20 Do the Mayan quiz. True (T) or False (F)?

1 The Aztecs built the modern day Mexico City on a lake called Texcoco because they saw a Quetzal bird there. T / **F**

2 The Mayas studied the Sun, the Moon and the stars to measure time. T / F

3 For the Aztecs, gold was the most important material in their lives. T / F

4 The Mayas used picture writing or 'glyphs' to communicate by writing. T / F

5 The Mayas played musical instruments. Some of these were made of turtle shells, wood and sea shells. T / F

6 The Pyramid of Kukulcan sounds like a Quetzal bird singing when someone climbs it. T / F

7 The Mayas played a ball game called Tlachtli. It's like a cross between modern volleyball and basketball. T / F

8 Aztec braves painted their faces and wore birds' feathers and animal fur to look beautiful and to make people love them. T / F

9 The first chewing gum was made from soft rubber from trees. The Mayas used it to clean their teeth. T / F

10 The form of a snake moves up and down the north stairs of the Pyramid of The Sun: up in March and down in September. T / F

Answers:
1 False. Because they saw an eagle there and thought it was a sign from their gods.
3 False. Quetzal feathers were more important than gold.
6 False. This happens when someone claps their hands.
8 False. They painted their faces and wore these things to look horrible and to make people feel afraid of them.

? Do you remember?

1 It's seven o'clock in the evening. Have you done your homework **yet?**_____

2 Yes, I've _____ finished it! I finished it ten seconds ago.

3 Paris is the _____ of France.

4 People in Mexico speak _____ .

5 North and south have got the same '_____' sound.

6 'What _____ are you?' 'I'm Portuguese.'

Can do   I can talk about what has already or just happened and what hasn't happened yet.   ☹ 😐 ☺

I can talk about different countries and nationalities.   ☹ 😐 ☺

I can complete a form in English.   ☹ 😐 ☺

1 Choose words from the box to complete the text.

Chinese	alphabet	started	~~book~~	days	people
for	Russia	important	years		

This (1) book__ is in the Latin alphabet. The people of Rome in Italy (2) _____ using the Latin alphabet more than two thousand seven hundred (3) _____ ago. Now more than two billion (4) _____ use it.

There are also a lot of other (5) _____ alphabets. After the Latin alphabet, the next most popular ways of writing are the Chinese script and the Devanagari alphabet from India. About 1.2 billion people use the (6) _____ script and 1 billion use the Devanagari alphabet. Then there is the Arabic alphabet, which is used by half a billion (five hundred million) people, and the Cyrillic alphabet. There are about 300 million people from Central and Eastern Europe, for example in (7) _____ , who use the Cyrillic alphabet. These are the most common alphabets but there are a lot of other ways of writing too.

2 Read again and answer.

1 What alphabet are you using to answer this question? The Latin alphabet._____
2 How old is it? _____
3 How many people use it today? _____
4 What alphabet do Indian people use? _____
5 What is the name of the other alphabet that people use in some Central and Eastern European countries? _____
6 How many people write in it? _____

3 Where are these English words from?

kiwi	kangaroo	karate	~~igloo~~	opera	athlete	chocolate

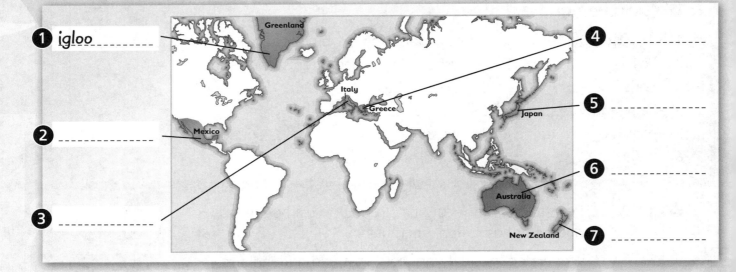

① igloo _____
② _____
③ _____
④ _____
⑤ _____
⑥ _____
⑦ _____

4 Read and think about prefixes. Write words 1–9 correctly.

Maskman is everyone's favourite hero because he's **(1) unkind** and **(2) unfriendly**. He's saved the world more than 20 times, which is very **(3) unexciting**. He's a **(4) microhero**. He can see things from a great distance because he's got **(5) microscopes** in his eyes. Not many people know that he almost never puts his clothes away at night. He's very **(6) tidy**. One day he couldn't find his mask and he had to save the world with a pair of tights on his head. Someone took a **(7) telegraph** of him wearing his new mask. He's got a copy of this **(8) usual** photo and when he looks at it, he laughs a lot and feels very **(9) unhappy**.

1 _Kind_____ 2 _____ 3 _____ 4 _____ 5 _____

6 _____ 7 _____ 8 _____ 9 _____

5 Read and answer.

Prefixes are things we can put at the front of a word to change its meaning. We also change words by adding things to the end of a word. These are called suffixes. Suffixes don't normally change the meaning. They change the grammar of the word.

Look at these suffixes.

| -s -er -est |
| -ed -ing |

Which ones can we use with the types of word below?

a adjectives ('small') _____

b verbs ('play') _-s,_____

c nouns ('pen') _-s,_____

Which suffix do we use for:

1 … present simple 'he', 'she', 'it' verbs? _-s___

2 … the person who does the action? _____

3 … verbs in continuous tenses? _____

4 … making plural nouns? _____

5 … verbs in the past? _____

6 … comparative adjectives? _____

7 … superlative adjectives? _____

Review Units 7 and 8

1 Read the story. Choose a word from the box. Write the correct word next to numbers 1–5.

| umbrellas | ~~just~~ | worn | Paris | belt | same | pockets | Spanish | capital | button |

Friendly

Dan, Alvin and Shari are sad because the second series of *Friendly* has **just** ended. They all agree that the funniest episode of this series was 'Jim's new clothes'.

In this episode Jim and Peter went to London to buy some new clothes. They caught the train to the **(1)** _____ one Saturday morning. They found a shop called Fine Fashion. The salesman told them that all the clothes came from **(2)** _____ , the capital of France and the capital of fashion.

Jim bought some big, green trousers with **(3)** _____ above the knees. He bought a light grey T-shirt and a black **(4)** _____ . He liked his new clothes and he decided to wear them home.

When they went back to the station, they saw Jim's grandfather, but it was very funny because his grandpa's trousers were big and green with pockets above the knees. He was also wearing a light grey T-shirt and a black belt. His clothes were the **(5)** _____ as Jim's.

2 Now choose the best name for the story.

Tick one box.

Streets ahead ☐   Capital cities ☐   The latest fashion ☐

3 Read and match the jokes.

1	What do you call an elephant at the North Pole?	a	Anything you want because it can't hear you!	☐
2	What did the scarf say to the hat?	b	A monkey!	☐
3	Why do birds fly south in winter?	c	A spoon!	☐
4	What must we break before we can use it?	d	Lost!	1
5	What kind of key opens a banana?	e	Because it's easier than walking!	☐
6	What do you get if you cross a kangaroo with an elephant?	f	Half way. Then you're walking out of the wood.	☐
7	What do you call an elephant with a carrot in each ear?	g	You go on ahead, I'll just hang around.	☐
8	What do sea monsters eat?	h	Big holes in Australia!	☐
9	How far can you walk into the wood?	i	An egg.	☐
10	What's the best thing to put into ice cream?	j	Fish and ships.	☐

4 Complete the sentences. Count and write the letters.

1 <u>Shorts</u> _____ are short trousers. We wear them in summer. `6`

2 Hindi, French and Portuguese are different _____ . ☐

3 We wear _____ on our hands. ☐

4 A hundred years is a _____ . ☐

5 He's just _____ his coat on. He's going out. ☐

6 Africa is a _____ . ☐

7 You might have a _____ inside your jacket. You can carry things in it. ☐

8 The cities of London, Paris and Rome are all _____ . ☐

9 We use this to close our shirts and coats. It can be different shapes and colours. _____ ☐

10 We wear a _____ at the top of our trousers or jeans so they don't fall down. ☐

11 'What _____ is she?' 'She's Chinese.' ☐

12 Oh, no! It's just started to rain and I've left my _____ at home! ☐

13 Women and girls wear _____ on their legs in cold weather. They aren't trousers or jeans. ☐

14 Special clothes to protect us. A firefighter wears one. _____ ☐

5 Now complete the crossword. Write the message.

s h o r t s

| 1 | 2 | 3 | 4 | 5 | 6 | | 7 | 4 | 6 | 7 |

h ☐ h !

6 Quiz time!

1 Why was Dan's shirt funny at the disco? <u>It was</u> _____

2 How long have people in China worn Han clothes? _____

3 What were moccasins? _____

4 How many countries won the ezine competition? _____

5 Where is sushi from? _____

6 What does the prefix 'tele-' mean? _____

7 Write questions for your quiz in your notebook.

Thanks and Acknowledgements

Authors' thanks

Many thanks to everyone at CUP, particularly to Maria Pylas, Susan Norris and Liane Grainger, and also to Hilary Ratcliff, for achieving such high standards throughout the 6 levels. All their vision and energy is clearly reflected on every page. We would also like to give a special mention to Gemma Wilkins and the Production team for all their hard work.

For level 6, our thanks go to Pippa Mayfield for her thoroughly good editing and joviality.

As always, we would like to thank John Green and Tim Woolf for their fine audio production and Rob Lee for his excellent songs.

A special thanks to all the pupils and teachers at Star English, El Palmar, Murcia for their help, suggestions and support at various stages of the project.

We would like to dedicate this book to our very good friend and colleague, Jim Kelly, for walking alongside us throughout the whole project and offering unlimited help and encouragement every step of the way.

The publishers are grateful to the following for permission to reproduce copyright photographs and material:

Alamy pp18 (Businessman/PhotoAlto), pp18 (tourist/Jupiterimages/BananaStock), pp36 (popcorn/Andrew Twort), pp36 (sauce boat/Westend61 GmbH), pp54 (raper/Bettina Strenske), pp54 (jumper/Andy Day), pp57 (court/Andrea Di Martino), pp64 (pocket/Oote Boe Photography), pp69 (goalkeeper/Kuttig - People), pp69 (dancer/PhotoAlto); Corbis UK Ltd. pp54 (seamstress/gLwa-Stephen Welstead), pp57 (hoop/Ludovic Maisant), pp69 (skier/Cultura), pp69 (hockey/Glyn Jones); dkimages.com pp54 (skateboard/Howard Shooter), pp54 (bicycle/Andy Crawford), pp64 (umbrella/Dave King), pp64 (gloves), pp64 (tights/Dave King), pp68cr (loom/De Agostini Editore Picture); Getty Images pp68/69 (fabric/Shelly Strazis/UperCut Images), pp69 (golfer/George Doyle & Ciaran Griffin/Stockbyte); NASA pp18 (astronaut), (moon walk/Kennedy Space Center), pp22 (earth), pp23 (volcano on Mars); Photolibrary Group pp51 (Parrotfish/Georgie Holland/age fotostock), pp51 (Butterflyfish/JW.Alker/imagebroker.net); Shutterstock pp18 (engineer/Hugo de Wolf), pp36 (wok/mates), pp36 (jam/Fribus Ekaterina), pp36 (chips/Harris Shiffman), pp36 (chopsticks/Emelyanov), pp54 (chess/Karen Struthers), pp63 (jeans/Vinnikava Viktoryia); Zooid Pictures pp36 (butter/Ned Dyke-Coomes), pp36 (Biscuit/Ned Dyke-Coomes), pp63 (scarf/Antonina Calabrese/Ned Dyke-Coomes), pp63 (cap/Ned Dyke-Coomes), pp63 (sock/Ned Dyke-Coomes), pp64 (button/Ned Dyke-Coomes), pp64 (shorts/Ned Dyke-Coomes), pp68 (needle/Ned Dyke-Coomes), pp68 (thread/Ned Dyke-Coomes), pp68 (cloth/Ned Dyke-Coomes).

The authors and publishers are grateful to the following illustrators:

FLP; Graham Kennedy; Gywneth Williamson; Jo Taylor, c/o Sylvie Poggio; Lisa Smith, c/o Sylvie Poggio; Mark Duffin; Mel Sharp, c/o Sylvie Poggio; Mike Phillips; Moreno Chiacchiera, c/o Beehive; Phil Burrows

The publishers are grateful to the following contributors:

Stephen Bond: commissioned photography
Hilary Fletcher: picture research
Pentacor**big**: concept design, cover design, book design and page make-up
Jo Taylor: cover illustration
John Green and Tim Woolf, TEFL Tapes: audio recordings
Robert Lee: song writing